SIKHIM

SIKHIM.

WITH HINTS ON

MOUNTAIN AND JUNGLE WARFARE.

EXHIBITING ALSO THE FACILITIES FOR OPENING COMMERCIAL RELATIONS THROUGH THE STATE OF SIKHIM WITH CENTRAL ASIA, THIBET, AND WESTERN CHINA.

BY

COLONEL J. C. GAWLER, F.R.G.S.

GYAN

Published by

Gyan Publishing House
5, Ansari Road
Daryaganj, New Delhi-110002
Phone: 011-47034999, 9811692060
E-mail: books@gyanbooks.com

Distribution Network
gyanbooks.com
India, USA, Canada, UK, Australia

ISBN: 8888-00-1000-463 (HB)
First Published, 1873

2nd Impression 2024

Printed at: Gyan Press, Delhi.

SIKHIM
Author: COLONEL J. C. GAWLER

E. Stanford Charing Cross.

"NOT AT ALL !, WHAT DO YOU MEAN BY IMPRACTICABLE"?

Introd. P.IV.

SIKHIM.

WITH HINTS ON

MOUNTAIN AND JUNGLE WARFARE.

EXHIBITING ALSO THE FACILITIES FOR OPENING COMMERCIAL RELATIONS THROUGH THE STATE OF SIKHIM WITH CENTRAL ASIA, THIBET, AND WESTERN CHINA.

Despatches published by permission of The Right Hon. the Secretary of State for India.

BY

COLONEL J. C. GAWLER, F.R.G.S.,

LATE 73RD REGIMENT,

KEEPER OF THE CROWN JEWELS, FORMERLY DEPUTY ADJUTANT-GENERAL, QUEEN'S TROOPS IN INDIA.

With Map and Illustrations.

" *V'thoaphoth hareem lo.*"

LONDON:

EDWARD STANFORD, 6 & 7, CHARING CROSS, S.W.

1873.

INTRODUCTION.

These Papers are published—

1. As a tribute to the officers and men of the Sikhim Field Force, whose heartiness, energy, and excellent conduct were in the highest degree instrumental in bringing to a successful and happy termination a campaign which, for the time it lasted, was pronounced by competent judges to have been as hard a bit of work as they had ever seen.

2. Because, from its geographical position, as well as from the complete success which crowned the expedition, Sikhim has been recently brought before the public as offering special facilities for opening commercial relations with Thibet, Central Asia, and Western China.

3. Because they contain a fair list of matters which would come under the consideration of the Officer in command of a force, whether independent or otherwise, particularly in a mountainous country.

They exhibit no brilliant novelty in strategy or tactics. "Never take a position in front which you "can gain by turning," is the old rule to which the force is possibly indebted for having suffered so little loss. And the British rule of measuring an enemy by his *fighting front*, conversely estimating what force is required by the space in which both sides may be limited to act, enabled me to employ small parties, which moved with ease and rapidity by different routes, disconcerting the enemy, and affording each other a true mutual support not to be attained by the single route and long tail.

Where mankind live, however dense the country may be, there must *at least* be footpaths for wood, water, and intercommunication.

As regards perseverance against the apparently impracticable, I may mention that, in the Kaffir War, when acting as Deputy Assistant Quartermaster-General to a column under my commanding officer the late Sir William Eyre, who afterwards commanded a division in the Crimea with much distinction, I was ordered by him to ride forward and see if the path which we were following on the top of the Buffalo range was practicable for the pack-horses. I did so, and ascertained that the plateau ended abruptly in a "krantz" or precipice, but that the footpath led to two rocks about four feet high, which allowed scarcely space enough for a man to pass, and descended immediately between them almost precipitously for fifteen or twenty feet, with forest trees and underwood below. I returned, and reported it "impracticable for pack-horses." "Not at all!" was the stern reply, "what do you mean by impracticable?" "I mean that they can't get down." "Not at all! Forward!" "Oh, of course you can roll them down." "Then they must roll."

It was a marvel to see the saddle-horses get down, the colonel leading the way. I remained to see all clear. The colonel's pack-horse advanced, and thrust its neck between the rocks; then without hesitation, standing on its hind-legs, it struggled forward until its load was caught on the tops of the two rocks; "shifting ballast for'ard," it went head first, turned over in the air, and amid shouts of laughter landed on the colonel's coffee-pot, which occupied a prominent position on the top of the load, and which appeared to be thereby rendered unfit for further service. The poor horse got up, the groom pushed the load straight, and continued the march as if nothing had happened. The other pack-horses performed it without falling, except the medical pack, the boxes of which seemed to give the animal less chance than a more yielding load.

Since then, observation and experience have convinced me that there are very few places where a man can *walk* that are impracticable for a horse.

TOWER, *September 7th*, 1873.

CONTENTS.

CHAPTER I.

CHAPTER II.

CHAPTER III.

CHAPTER IV.

CHAPTER V.

APPENDIX.

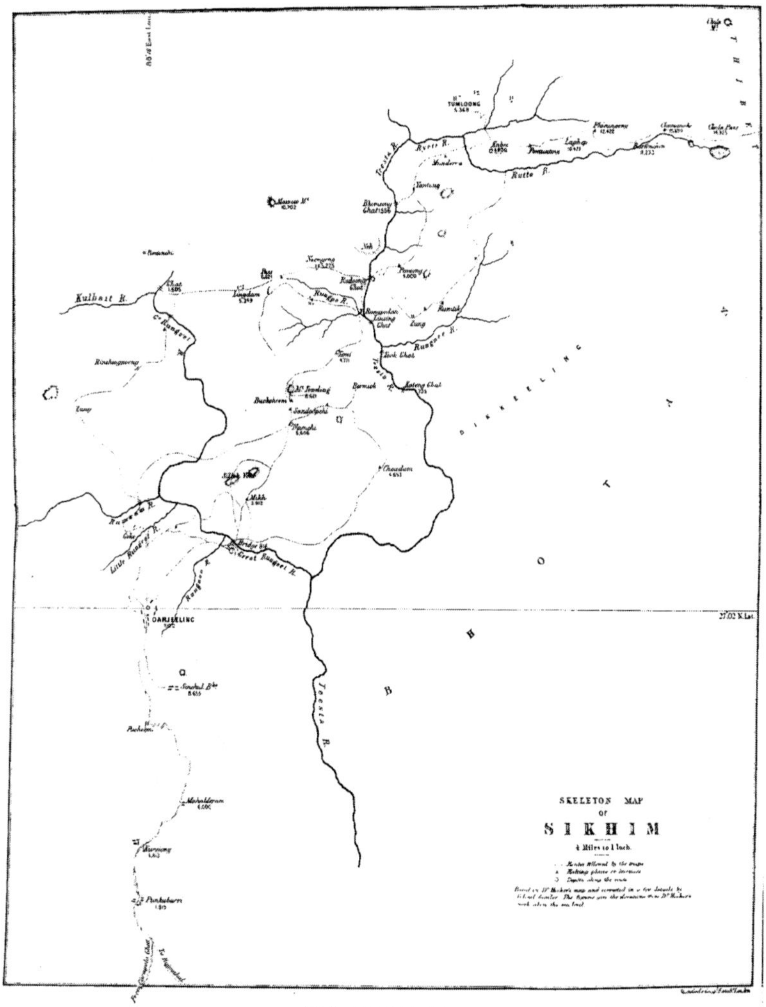

London: Edward Stanford, 6 & 7, Charing Cross, S.W.

SIKHIM.

CHAPTER I.

Appointment — Force — Dr. Hooker's work — condition of Darjeeling — previous military history of Sikhim — remarks on bush fighting—Letter, December 24th, 1860, foreign relations—composition of population—cause of quarrel—proceedings of Government—disaster—topography, rivers, roads, climate, &c.—transport—proposed operations—miscellaneous—statement of supplies.

On the evening of the 12th December, 1860, when in command of the Recruit Depôt, at Dum Dum, near Calcutta, I received a telegram from the Quartermaster-General of the Army, through the General commanding the Presidency Division, directing me, by order of His Excellency Sir Hugh Rose, Commander-in-Chief, to proceed to Darjeeling to take command of all the troops at that station, and of a field force, as per margin, which was to be assembled there. The telegram continued, "He may select his "own staff, and is authorized to "make full and complete ar-"rangements for the organiza-"tion and supply of the troops under his command,

ORIGINAL FORCE.

	Officers.	Rank and File.
Convalescent Depôt (European)	3	130
Native troops ..	6	190
1 mountain gun.		

REINFORCEMENTS.

Royal Artillery ..	1	20
2 Naval Brigade howitzers.		
1 Mountain battery.		
H.M. 6th Royal Regt.		400
73rd N.I., 5 companies.		450
3rd Sikh infantry, 1 wing.		450
Sikh police		290

RESERVE.

(At Titalyah.)

H.M. 19th Regt., 3 companies.
Mynpoorie levy, 3 companies.

(At Julpigoree.)

Mynpoorie levy, 2 companies.
Benares Horse, 3 troops.

(At Purneah.)

Bhagulpore Rangers, 1 wing.

"as well as to obtain information in connection with "the service he may be employed on." Such orders were liberal and wide enough for anyone.

I had been at the foot of the Himalayas, but never into them, and I knew that Darjeeling was a civil station and invalid depôt nearly due north of Calcutta.

I went into Calcutta the next day to lay my dâk, and to learn what I could about the troops and stores already at Darjeeling, and those that had just been put in motion. Calling on that gallant and excellent officer, the late Sir J. Hearsay, then commanding the Presidency Division, I was advised by him to procure 'Hooker's Himalayan Journals,' and to read it on my way up. I bought a copy, and started on the evening of the 14th. I took with me a pack-saddle which had done me good service at the Cape, two solid leather expanding portmanteaus, 18 in. × 12 in., for which I had straps and rings to sling them on the pack-saddle,* blankets, and a piece of tarpaulin which had served me many a time.

My route was by rail to Rajmahal, where there was a steam-ferry, and thence by palkee dâk from Maldah, about 120 miles, to Punkabarri (1815 feet), at the foot of the hills. From this point the hill road commenced, and, after a steep zig-zag ascent to Kursiong (4813 feet), continued for 36 miles of a good

* I afterwards had made at Darjeeling two cane baskets to fit the pack-saddle. They were sufficiently stiff to keep their contents from being crushed or broken, as sometimes happens with saddle-bags, and yet more yielding than boxes, and less likely than either to be broken or torn open. The weather would be fine, and the tarpaulin would keep out all the damp we were likely to have.

though narrow road (I think the width was 12 feet) to Darjeeling (7100 feet).

I reached Darjeeling, and saw the many snowy peaks of Kinchinjunga, varying from 20,000 to 28,000 feet, lighted up by the sun before it was really daylight at the spot where I stood! The magnificent mass seemed within two miles of me, instead of forty.

I could not fail to be impressed with the grandeur of the scenery, but on such points I must refer anyone to Dr. Hooker, and stick to that which came within my province, *viz.* the consideration of all these snowy peaks, deep dark valleys, foaming torrents, and interminable forests in relation to roads, means of transport, and expenditure of shoe leather.

As Sir James Hearsay had predicted, I found Dr. Hooker's work invaluable. Never was the officer commanding a force favoured with a fuller, more able, or more lucid report of a country and its inhabitants than I was by the study of Dr. Hooker.

I found the inhabitants of Darjeeling looking out anxiously for reinforcements. The enemy were occasionally patrolling our territory and even threatening our communications with Punkabarri.

In 1789 the people of Sikhim had repulsed the Nepalese, who, in turn, had, in the war of 1815, repulsed two out of three of our columns. So recently as 1849, moreover, Sikhim had been pronounced "impracticable for British troops," which opinion was concurred in by Sir C. Napier, then Commander-in-Chief ('Life of Sir C. Napier,' vol iv., p. 240), but the old hero was then probably feeling aged and weary.

"In a precipitous and densely-wooded country like "this," said the Military Report, dated January 1st, 1850, on the strength of which the expedition was abandoned, "where the track is with difficulty traced "through an almost impenetrable jungle of brush- "wood and briars, with the largest forest trees on "either side of it,* the facility with which the best "troops may be impeded, if not entirely stopped, by "the felling of forest trees across the path without "any necessity of firing a shot, is so evident that "further remark is unnecessary. It is not a belt of "forest to be passed through, or a pass to be forced; "the whole country presents but one feature."

The ability of the British soldier to cope with the savage or an uncivilized enemy in the bush is always liable to be questioned by some who are either inexperienced or who have not thoroughly tried it; and, in engaging in this style of warfare, regiments who are new to it are confronted with circumstances so novel, that they often purchase their experience dearly unless they are first sent in company with older hands, or are possessed of an inventive Com-

* From 12,000 to 10,000 feet are found the fir, dwarf rhododendron, cherry, pear, dwarf bamboo, primroses, and violets.

From 10,000 to 9000 feet, oak, chestnut, magnolia, rhododendron, olive, fig, maple, cheem bamboo, nettles.

From 8000 to 6500 feet, elder, peach, oak, chestnut, maple, walnut, olive, birch, holly, raspberry, strawberry, magnolia, all the English flowers, potato, brambles.

From 8000 to 3000 feet, magnolia, maple, rhododendron, oak, laurels, lime-trees.

5000 feet is about the upper limit of cultivation for rice, barley, buckwheat, Indian corn, yam, mint, and rue.

From 4000 to 1000 feet, cotton, banian, fig, oranges, peaches, banana, lemon.—*From Revenue Survey Map of Darjeeling Territory.*

manding Officer, who is animated with "the will to "do and soul to dare."

At the outbreak of the Kaffir War of 1850–3, I have heard a whole mess-table of officers of considerable experience argue hotly against the officer commanding the 73rd Regiment, the late Sir William Eyre, who as hotly expressed his intention of making his men fight in the bush, *i. e.* enter the bush after the Kaffirs. "You'll get your regiment cut to "pieces;" "You'll get an assegai into you;" "Im-"possible!" "Absurd!" "English soldiers can't do "it;" were some of the principal assertions. Colonel Eyre's argument was, "If the well-armed, well-shod, "disciplined, and well-fed British soldier is not a "match for a savage anywhere, *in the bush or out of* "*it*, the sooner we give up the country the better." His regiment was well in hand, and Colonel Eyre very soon proved the correctness of his views. The spell was broken, and most regiments that served in the Kaffir War of 1850–3 could skirmish well through any bush; and Cape bush, for timber, brambles, thorns, monkey rope, and other underwood and tanglement, yields to none.

In bush fighting, as in all other, the considerations are moral and physical.

A savage prefers the bush because he would rather not meet his foe in the open. To induce him to fight, it is a *sine quâ non* that he should have large odds of some description on his side, and this he generally tries to effect by being in concealment himself while his foe is exposed. His fondest wishes are therefore thoroughly gratified by any officer who, when attacked, keeps his men outside the bush. But, if the officer turns the discipline of his men to account, and dashes with them into the bush, the necessary fighting odds of the savage are at once reduced, and the soldier is every moment on more even terms with him, to try him at close quarters if he will stand, which he never does.

The Kaffirs have a proverb, "Two men can't stop "in the same bush," *i. e.* if one persists in coming in the other had better go out! It may require a moral effort for men in the open, or on a path, to dash at a concealed enemy, but consideration and practice will prove its soundness and efficacy.

Even superior numbers of savages will run, for they lack that dependence on one another which discipline bestows. I must lay a stress on *discipline*, for I have witnessed among Kaffirs individual acts of gallantry and devotion unsurpassed by any race.

As to the physical considerations, it is a mistake to suppose that a savage can run like a rabbit through miles of underwood as thick as a quickset hedge. He will hide himself in such from pursuit, or he will, *if the chance be given him*, waylay you, with great sense and judgment, from behind a narrow strip of almost impenetrable thicket; but *he has crept there from some neighbouring path*, and a general dash at it soon reveals some practicable holes, as well as where it terminates, and the savages run by the clearest route to avoid being caught in their own trap.

The 73rd, as well as many other regiments, lost many a trouser leg, hat, or sleeve of a coat at such places; but as Colonel Eyre never allowed himself to be surprised, and, as he frequently turned the tables and waylaid the Kaffirs, his regiment met with none of the disasters which were experienced by most others during the first part of the war, and the enemy always ran.

As to the relative ability of the clothed or unclothed man to make his way through the jungle where there is no path, I found when, subsequent to the war of 1850–3, I commanded Kaffirs on active service, that the unshod and half-clad savage has a very great dislike to leaving the footpath for the unbeaten bush, particularly if it be wet from rain or dew. It tears his skin, and thick though they be, the soles of his feet become spongy with wet, and are soon penetrated by thorns. I have often seen Kaffirs who have had a pair of hide shoes, lend one of them as the greatest favour on the importunity of a bosom friend, and thus both of them have trudged along with one shoe apiece, and then changed them so that each foot might have a turn!

The intellectual part of bush tactics is only the exercise of the animal instincts and intelligence, which the uneducated savage possesses; and, with a little practice, where should be found men more apt for border raid, or "hunting craft by lake and wood," than the countrymen of Robin Hood or bold Rob Roy?

The following letters to the Quarter-Master-General form a sort of journal of events and matters as they presented themselves to me:—

To the Qr. Mast. General of the Army.

SIR, DARJEELING, DEC. 24TH, 1860.

I have the honour to acknowledge the receipt yesterday of your letter of instructions, dated Fyzabad, 13th December, 1860, with enclosures; and, as I see by the copy of your letter to the Secretary of Government of the same date, that His Excellency the Commander-in-Chief had not then been informed of the character and locality of the operations, and the object and intention of the Government in connection with the movements in Sikhim, I will briefly relate the circumstances antecedent to and attending the recent disturbances; and, as no instructions have as yet been received by Dr. Campbell, Governor-General's Agent, I trust I may be excused entering upon politics in endeavouring to calculate what measures the Government are likely to take, that I may be able to submit to His Excellency the Commander-in-Chief information, and propositions for the attainment of our object.

I annex a map of the country, taken from travels by Dr. Hooker, to which Dr. Campbell has often referred for information, and which I read through on my journey up.

FOREIGN RELATIONS.—The State of Sikhim was rescued from the encroachments of Nepaul some forty years ago, and has remained a *protégé* of the British Government ever since. It is bounded on the north and east by Thibet, with which country it has some intimate relations. The head of the religion (Bhudism) is in Thibet; the Rajah's wife is a Thibetean; the Dewan is a Thibetean; and both the Rajah and the Dewan frequently reside in Thibet at Choombi, eastward of the Chola Pass. The Rajah receives a stipend from the Thibet Government for assisting them to keep the passes. He is old and imbecile. The Dewan is over the middle age, avaricious and insolent, a monopolizer of trade, and feared and disliked by the people.

COMPOSITION, &c., OF POPULATION.—The population of Sikhim is made up of several tribes; Lepchas and Limboos, who reside principally west of the Great Rungeet, are mild, inoffensive, hardworking, and fond of the English; Sikhim Bhooteas, who are rude and insolent, but likewise hardworking. East of the Teesta are several Thibeteans; they are all hardy, and their physical powers are immense. Unlike the Hindoos, their priests will eat anything you give them. There is no "caste." They are armed with bows and poisoned arrows and a few guns.*

CAUSES OF QUARREL AND PROCEEDINGS OF GOVERNMENT. —So long ago as March last, some subjects of the Rajah of Sikhim, who eventually turned out to be relations of the Dewan, kidnapped on various occasions, within the British territory, subjects of the British Government. Restitution was demanded by us, and no satisfactory answer received. After several months the British Government directed the occupation, for three months, of a strip of territory belonging to the Sikhim Rajah, lying between the Great Rungeet on the east, and, the boundary of Nepaul on the west, and if restitution of British subjects was not made within that period, the strip was to be permanently annexed.

Temporary possession was taken of the country on the 1st November, 1860, by the Superintendent of Darjeeling and a body of Sebundy Sappers under command of Captain Murray. They cut roads and commenced establishing themselves at Rinchingpoong. The people of the country assisted them with good will, and the expedition even collected supplies through the aid of the Sikhim authorities.

They were, however, attacked on the 27th November by a mixed force of Thibeteans and Sikhim Bhooteas, under

* This was a mistake. Thibeteans and Bhooteas all had guns.

direction of the Dewan, and were compelled to retreat. They had received notice on the 21st November that they were to be attacked, and, had the Lepchas and Limboos proved hostile, they must have been cut to pieces. The roads were damaged on their line of retreat, they were waylaid, and rocks rolled upon them. The Sebundy Sappers, who hardly knew how to use their guns, disappeared in all directions.

Dr. Campbell, Captain Murray, and Lieut. Beavan, 73rd N.I., made their way to Darjeeling with only two attendants. Serjeant Jones and a few others came in the next day, and for several days the sappers dropped in by twos and threes, many without their arms, which had been either lost or thrown away to enable them to pass as coolies. There are still one Havildar and nineteen Sepoys missing or prisoners; and property in the hands of the enemy as per margin.

1 3-pounder gun complete.
40 Cartridges for ditto.
16 Round shot.
8 Case shot.
70 Grooved rifles.
67 Sets accoutrements.
103 Rifle swords & scabbards.
9000 Rnds. rifle ammunition.
250 Hoes.
25 Pickaxes.
25 Felling axes.
2 Sets miners' tools.
1 Case mathematical instruments.
Bedding.
Sundry stores.

To punish the State of Sikhim for its original aggression and subsequent treachery is only part of the consideration. The remainder being to do it in such a way as shall vindicate our honour, and counteract the political effect which such a string of plunder, as appears in the margin, will have upon Thibet and Bhotan. Subjects of the former country were employed against us, and to the latter State the Dewan is holding out a bribe of a strip of territory on their border, called "Dikkeeling," if they will assist him.

The mere reoccupation of the original piece of territory taken by us, and perhaps an additional piece, would entail two or more standing camps, whose communications with Darjeeling would require to be kept up by smaller posts and continual escorts. Roads might be made and the country thus opened, but it would, I think, lead only to our camps and escorts being continually harassed at the enemy's pleasure; or, as before, he might affect satisfaction at our presence and endeavour to lull us into security to make a better sweep. I am assured that, had the attack been a fortnight later, several ladies and children would now probably be in the hands of the enemy.

It is therefore with the conviction that it would ensure the future comfort and security of the troops and country that I venture to express the hope that the instructions from Government will be to give the enemy his first lesson in "Tumloong," his capital, and if necessary to destroy it, previous to occupying or reoccupying any portion of his territory. The same course was proposed in 1849, when the same Dewan made prisoners of Drs. Campbell and Hooker, in hopes of forcing something out of the British Government. This insult, offered to the Governor-General's Agent near the Chola Pass, almost within sight of the Thibet guard, went unpunished. A force was assembled at Darjeeling, but the country was pronounced to be "impracticable for British troops," although there were plenty of volunteers for the service. The Dewan, however, was disgraced, and the Lhassa authorities threatened to send him bound to the Emperor of China, for so nearly embroiling them with the British Government.

"Considering, however, his energy," wrote Dr. Hooker in 1854, "a rare quality in these countries, I should not be "surprised at his yet cutting a figure in Bhotan, *if not in* "*Sikhim itself*."—(Hooker's 'Himalayan Journals,' vol. ii., p. 241.)

TOPOGRAPHY, ASPECT, &c.—In the accompanying map the mountains, rivers, towns, &c., are, I am assured by Dr. Campbell, very accurately placed; but the aspect of the country is by no means conveyed. The rivers lie *very* deep, and the ascents out of them for the first 1000 feet are almost precipitous (even by the paths, which usually follow the ridges), after which the slope is considerably less until near the summit of the range.

The ranges, to which our operations would be confined, are at a lower elevation than Darjeeling (7000 feet), mostly covered with forest trees, which afford excellent firewood. There is no malaria in the jungles, except in summer time in the beds of some of the rivers.

RIVERS AND BRIDGES.—The rivers are rapid;* the Teesta is about 80 yards broad; there are fords, but not many. Rafts are constructed by a few coolies in a few hours; or a cane suspension bridge (which horses or cattle can cross) in about a week.

ROADS.—Except the roads cut by Dr. Campbell on the west of the Great Rungeet, there are only foot paths in the country. Horses and cattle do, however, travel on many of them; there are two practicable paths for horses and cattle to Tumloong.

CLIMATE.—The ranges between this and Tumloong are lower than Darjeeling, and not so cold.

SEASON.—There is usually a little dullness, and perhaps rain, late in December and early in January, after which it remains bright until May, when a few storms and rains set in, which increasing in force may last until October.

RESOURCES OF THE COUNTRY.—The country produces but sufficient grain for its own consumption: wheat, buckwheat,

* According to Dr. Hooker's measurement, the Rungeet, in a course of 23 miles between the Ghât above the Kulhait River and that at the cane bridge below Darjeeling, falls 987 feet. The Teesta, between the Bhomsong and Katong Ghâts, a course of between 10 and 12 miles, falls 821 feet. *Vide* also Captain Impey's Report, para. 15 (Appendix); the Teesta was running at 14 miles between the rocks.

yellow millet, Indian corn, and a little rice. Plantains and oranges are grown. There are cattle, but not in any very great numbers. Both cattle and ponies are imported from Thibet. There is no lack of timber or bamboo; of the latter the natives speedily make with a few strokes of their long straight heavy knives, either chair, table, bed, bucket, or house.*

TRANSPORT.—Coolies are used as the principal means of transport in the enemy's country; they carry incredible loads, but the ordinary travelling load is about 80 lbs. (eighty). There will be a scarcity of coolies at first, until we have re-established our reputation, but large numbers of ponies can be obtained from the plains; they will, however, only assist, not supersede, the coolies until roads are made.

PROPOSED OPERATIONS.—Should an advance on Tumloong be decided on, leaving 400 men to garrison Darjeeling, I would move on to Namchi, under Mount Tendong, which, although only about 12 miles as the crow flies, and plainly visible from Darjeeling, it would take three days at least for the force and supplies to reach. Namchi is a very healthy place, not so cold as Darjeeling, and the ridge on which it is situated is broad and flat. I would there form a strong

	Rank and File.
H.M. 6th Regiment ..	400
3rd Sikhs	400
73rd N.I.	420
Sikh police	290
Convalescent depôt ..	120
Sebundy Sappers	190
	1820

* The bamboos attain from 7 inches to 9 inches diameter.

Perhaps this is the most suitable place to mention the cane which rendered us such service in the construction of our bridges. It grows principally in bamboo jungle, and is about 1½ to 2 inches in diameter. I once traced a single piece for 80 yards, and then failed to find the end.

The jungles are infested with leeches, which penetrate loosely-woven clothes and deprive the wearer of a good deal of blood before he finds them out. They get far up the noses of horses, goats, &c., and cannot be removed without subjecting the poor animal to a couple of days without water, which, being afterwards offered to him, the leeches also want to drink, and may be seized. If allowed to remain, the animal becomes reduced to a skeleton.

camp, if I have the force I expect, and leaving 300 men to guard it, would proceed with the remainder to Tumloong, five marches more, either by the Bhomsong road or across the Took Ghât. I should prefer the latter road, as it would give me the chance of cutting off the enemy's communication with Thibet.*

MISCELLANEOUS.—The enemy are armed with bows and arrows and a few guns,† the greater part of which latter are those taken from Dr. Campbell's party. Their home-made ammunition is barely serviceable.

Rockets ‡ would, I think, be very useful here, and I have therefore written for some, and also for three mortars belonging to the Mountain Train Battery, which had been left behind.

I have also desired the Commissariat Officer to lay in tobacco and more rum, as the Sikhs wish to open a canteen.

I annex a copy of answers by the Commissariat Officer to certain questions which I sent him on the day of my arrival, with reference to supplies.

I have indented for a supply of axes, hatchets, &c., which I propose issuing to the different corps, at a proportion per company. I trust His Excellency the Commander-in-Chief will approve of this and give orders that it may be complied with.

There is a large quantity of hemp here, and I have given directions to Captain Murray to have some strong cable and rope made to enable us to construct a better bridge over the Rungeet.

I am well satisfied with the force the Commander-in-Chief

* As time progressed I thought less of the enemy, but found my transport very limited, and moreover of a very delicate constitution. The two first obliged and allowed me to proceed with a smaller force; the last obliged me to change my route, so as to give the Bhotan frontier a wide berth, and to enable me to cross the Teesta at a nearer point to Tumloong—(*Vide* p. 50).

† *Vide* note, p. 9. ‡ *Vide* p. 80.

has given me, and the powers for organization with which he has invested me. I see plenty of hard work, but nothing insurmountable.

The only link where there seems likely to be a hitch, is in the transport between Rajmahal and the foot of the hills. I have requested the officer in charge of the commissariat at Rajmahal to keep me informed of the stores there awaiting transport, and likewise the dates of their despatch from thence.

I have, &c.,

JOHN C. GAWLER,

Lieut.-Colonel, Commanding Troops at Darjeeling.

Queries addressed to Commissariat Officer, and replies:—

QUERIES.	REPLIES.
What quantity of slaughter cattle (sheep and oxen) have the commissariat or contractor? Are any expected? In what length of time may they be expected after an order leaves this?	About forty bullocks and thirty sheep in hand; the supply of meat at present by Government agency; from the 1st proximo by contract. Cattle are being purchased in anticipation of the arrival of the contractors. The contractors are bound to keep at all times one month's supply on hand. Three months' stock shall be completed within fifteen days.
What biscuit is there in hand? and is it in bags or barrels? What is expected, and when? Are the troops eating bread or biscuit?	Between 200 lbs. and 300 lbs. 12,000 lbs. despatched from Calcutta; it is believed that 9000 lbs. have been sent with the first detachment 6th Foot, *en route* for Darjeeling. The troops are eating bread, supplied by contract to the end of the year, by Government agency, from the 1st proximo.

Queries.	Replies.
What quantity of flour is there? Where is flour procurable? In what time can it be obtained?	About 60 maunds of soojee in hand. 60 maunds despatched from Caragola will be received before the end of the month, and 60 more maunds despatched from Monghir. Several agents engaged in purchasing; 300 maunds soojee ordered from Calcutta by rail to Rajmahal, as soon as it was known that additional troops were coming to Darjeeling.
Ditto, ditto rice and other grain?	About 30 maunds of rice for Europeans. Flour chiefly procurable from Monghir. It can be had in small quantities from Purneah and Maldah. At both places soojee is now being prepared. Rice can be had in larger quantities from Kishnigunge.
What weight of meat is there in an ordinary sized bullock? Ditto, ditto, sheep?	Average weight of a hill bullock, 200 lbs.; of a sheep, 20 lbs. Orders for all necessary supplies consequent on the increase of troops at Darjeeling have already been given.

JOHN C. GAWLER,
Lt.-Col. Commanding.

(Signed) E. T. FITZGERALD,
A. A. C. Gen.

DARJEELING,
22*nd Dec.*, 1860.

CHAPTER II.

Letter, January 1st, 1861, stockades at the Rungeet—instructions from Government—6th Royal Regiment—January 14th, the mortar question—January 17th, force assembled—supplies—transport—position of the enemy—miscellaneous—statement of supplies—crowding of stores at the foot of the hills—insufficient transport—description of ground at Rungeet bridge—January 26th and 28th, letters about transport—30th January, coolie corps—wishes regarding bridge at Rungeet—opposition of the enemy—two men wounded—arrangements for crossing.

To the Qr. Mast. General of the Army.

SIR, DARJEELING, JAN. 1ST, 1861.

I have the honour to report, in continuation, that on the 28th ultimo I proceeded to the Rungeet River to examine some stockades, said to have been constructed and enlarged on the enemy's side of the river, near the site of the old Rungeet bridge, a little below the junction of the Rungnoo.

I had the day before sent down a party of Sebundy Sappers, under Lieutenant Beavan, to make a bridge over the Rungnoo, in anticipation of future operations. The sappers are protected during the day by a covering party of the 73rd N.I., detached from the Rungeet Guard, and by patroles from the Rungeet and Pushook Guards along the south bank of the river.

The bed of the Rungeet is, at the old bridge, about 90 yards in width, but the river does not at this season occupy more than 40 yards. The enemy's stockades are placed along the bank on their own side. They consist of stone walls faced with green bamboo, in some places three-deep, and loop-holed. They cannot be enfiladed from our side. I imagine that they have only been constructed in anticipation of our attempting to cross. About fifteen or twenty of the enemy watched my proceedings from their stockades and from the higher ground, but did not offer to molest me. I caused a few bamboos, with which they had, since Major Maitland's visit, endeavoured to make a foot bridge, to be cut away, as I did not wish to leave them the power of destroying our work at the Rungeet.

Dr. Campbell received instructions this morning to re-occupy the territory to the west of the Great Rungeet, in such a manner that a force shall be able to advance upon Tumloong. There will be some delay in crossing the boundary, as Dr. Campbell desires first to be able to tell the natives whether the country is to be permanently annexed or only occupied temporarily. In the former case the real natives of the country (Lepchas and Limboos) would render us every assistance, and in the latter they would be afraid to risk the consequences from their masters, the Bhooteas and Thibeteans.

I have decided, however, with Dr. Campbell's concurrence, in collecting supplies at Goke,* which will be the gain of a day's march whenever an advance is ordered, as thence diverge the only two roads to the territory west of the Great Rungeet, and thence also a fair road, with an ascent easier than from the old Rungeet bridge, leads to Namchi, which I have fixed upon as the most favourable position for a principal depôt, in the event of an advance upon Tumloong.

Marching has already told sadly on the boots. The wing of the 6th Royals left Barrackpore with three good pairs per man, and when I inspected them on the 31st ultimo, many had already worn out two pairs.

* I was obliged to abandon this plan for want of transport.

I have written to the Presidency requesting a fresh supply, and for means and permission to establish a shoemaker's shop forthwith.

I have, &c.,

J. C. Gawler, Lt.-Col.

From Lieut.-Col. Gawler, commanding Troops, Darjeeling, to the Assist. Adjutant-General, Benares Division.

Sir, Darjeeling, Jan. 14th, 1861.

I have the honour to acknowledge the receipt of a letter, No. 1691, of the Commissary of Ordnance, Allahabad Arsenal, forwarded for my information, and regret that the Major-General should think that I intended incurring expense to Government in ignorance of the use of the arm for which I made application.

I did not apply for the mortars merely to increase my artillery, which for offensive purposes is more than I require, though not of the requisite description. I could not judge of this until I had seen the country, and this was not until after the despatch of the battery had been notified from Allahabad. And, as it had been ordered up by His Excellency the Commander-in-Chief, and would prove useful in the defence of camps, if the occupation only of the country were decided on, I did not feel justified in stopping them at any intermediate station.

Although mortars are not attached to the Hazara or Peshawur mountain train batteries, the Commissary of Ordnance admits that "they may be "found useful under particular circumstances," and that "the tactique of "mountain train artillery will vary according to the nature of the country," and I respectfully observe that the nature of the whole of this country embraces the whole of those circumstances, for several positions might occur in a day's march, whence the enemy, were he tolerably confident and well armed, could not be dislodged without the aid of mortars.

The small penetration mentioned by the Commissary of Ordnance is no objection, as the mortars are not required to destroy houses or magazines.

I have, &c.,

J. C. Gawler,

Lieut.-Col., commanding Troops, Darjeeling.

NOTE.—The mortars were afterwards forwarded by order of the Commander-in-Chief, but arrived too late to be of any service. We should have been sadly crippled for want of them if the enemy had stood at Neh. *Vide* p. 55.

To the Qr. Mast. General of the Army.

SIR, DARJEELING, JAN. 17TH, 1861.

I had the honour to report yesterday, for the information of His Excellency the Commander-in-Chief, the movement of troops, by which it will be seen that the whole force destined for Sikhim is now assembled. The mountain train battery ordered by His Excellency, however, was only to have left Caragola yesterday. The mortars belonging to it have not been sent, and my subsequent application for them has been refused. My reasons for wishing for them are contained in a letter to the Assistant Adjutant-General, Benares Division, annexed. There are present two 3-pr. guns, and two naval brigade 12-pr. howitzers, just received from Calcutta.

SUPPLIES.—Slaughter cattle, biscuits, rum, rice, &c., are in sufficient quantities for a good start. There is, however, little or no "atta," which is the chief food for Sikhs. A supply will be up in about three weeks, until which time mutton and rum, as recommended by the medical officers, will be issued to them, as rice and bhoota (Indian corn) alone make them sick.

Major FitzGerald, Deputy Commissary-General, arrived yesterday. I annex a statement of supplies.

TRANSPORT.—I am rather anxious about transport, *i. e.* sufficient for rapid movements. Dr. Campbell has also expressed some doubts about the coolies consenting to enter Sikhim, unless he is able to proclaim that the country is to be permanently annexed.

I am endeavouring, however, to bring matters to an issue, and beg to submit a memo. on the formation of a Coolie Corps, drawn up by Lieutenant Fryer, R.B., in which I fully concur.* I do not, however, think that the locomotive powers of a British force should depend upon what assistance the people of the country may be agreeable to afford; and, with rough insolent neighbours like the Bhotanese (although not avowed enemies at present), I think an establishment of mules should be kept up at this station; there would be plenty of occupation for them even if no hostilities were going on.

Captain Renny, 3rd Sikhs, has brought with him 35 Government mules and yaboos, and I annex a copy of a letter which I have written to the Division in the hopes of obtaining more.†

POSITION OF THE ENEMY.—The enemy are encamped at Namchi, a village which I have before mentioned as being visible from Darjeeling. According to Dr. Campbell's information there are about 800 there, with a few jingalls, some matchlocks, and the rifles and ammunition which they took from the first expedition. There are some Thibeteans amongst them, who are considered by the natives terrible, but only, so far as I can learn, from their wearing, as a head-

* I regret that I have no copy of this very able memo.

† Through a misapprehension either of my wishes or of the nature of the country, the ponies purchased were almost useless. Those procured were the half-starved, ragged hipped, undersized animals that are seen carrying bricks or sand in the plains, instead of the stout pony that is fit for anything. I purchased in Darjeeling, after my arrival, an excellent riding pony for Rs.100; a second, also fit for the saddle, but which I used for my pack, for Rs.60; and a young stout pony, as a second pack, for Rs.30. These did all my work without the aid of coolies. (*Vide* also pp. 28 and 64.)

dress, an inverted iron pot. They keep a picket of fifty or sixty men near their stockades, opposite the site of the old Rungeet bridge.

Dr. Campbell has lately suspected the Bhotanese of double dealing; first, from a letter that was sent to him anonymously, purporting to be from a Bhotan Soubah, and undoubtedly bearing his seal, to a native in the plains, asking for more powder, and for information concerning treasuries and the movement of troops towards Darjeeling; secondly, because Soubahs of Bhotan are now with the Dewan near Namchi. Should Dr. Campbell be of the same mind when we are about to advance, I shall strengthen our outposts, particularly that towards the Bhotan frontier, and order up two companies of Her Majesty's 19th Regt. and 200 men, Mynpooree levy, before quitting.

MISCELLANEOUS.—The rockets I applied for were despatched from Calcutta on the 2nd of this month, with a quantity of entrenching tools, which I indented for at the same time.

Five hundred pairs of boots for the wing, Her Majesty's 6th Regiment, were despatched from Calcutta on the 11th instant.

I inspected Renny's Sikhs yesterday, and was much pleased with their appearance; their arms, accoutrements, and their whole equipment were in admirable order. Their "posteens," however, were worn out in the plains, but great coats and blankets for them are now on their way from Calcutta.

I have, &c.,

JOHN C. GAWLER, Lieut.-Colonel,
Commanding Troops at Darjeeling.

P. S.—January 18th, The Hon. Ashley Eden, Envoy and Special Commissioner, arrived yesterday evening.

J. C. G.

Statement of stores at Darjeeling, Commissariat Godown, calculated for 500 Europeans :—

Tea, mixed ..	2065 lbs.	3 months.
Coffee	7539 „	5 „
Rum	2500 gallons ..	3 „
Biscuit*	8000 lbs.	16 days.

Sugar, salt, and rice procurable in the bazaar; hospital stores, wine, &c., in large quantities.

One month's supply of provisions for 1200 native troops (the ration consisting of rice); with the exception of Ghee, which is not yet complete.

(Signed) E. T. FitzGerald.

Darjeeling.

N.B.—A further stock of biscuit was at Punkabarri on the 14th, and some *en route* from Caragola.

John C. Gawler,
Lieut.-Colonel.

* Biscuit calculated for 500 Europeans; 350 only will be able to enter Sikhim, and, until the advance, the troops receive bread.

J. C. G.,
Lieut.-Colonel.

About this time difficulties seemed to begin. Troops and stores were converging on Punkabarri by two good roads, *viz.* from the Presidency *viâ* Rajmahal, and from the Benares Division *viâ* Caragola Ghât, while from Punkabarri to Darjeeling there was only the one narrow road of 36 miles, and coolies were the principal means of transport.

The storage room at Punkabarri was very small, and at Darjeeling it was by no means extensive.

This is an embarrassment likely to befall any force,

particularly at a point of disembarkation, or where civilization ends or their own primary arrangements terminate. There are quantities of stores either quite unsuited to the country, or of very secondary importance, or much in excess of what are required, that absorb transport and storage room, and come to hand in place of those which are urgently required.

The transport in the plains I afterwards learned was being strained to forward stores, and the animals were dying from fatigue.

So soon as I comprehended matters, I endeavoured to regulate the supplies from the fountain-head, and to stop at intermediate stations some stores that were in transit.

In addition to beef and mutton, which in the field find their own transport, I decided on biscuit, sugar, coffee, rum, and rice, as our staple requirements in Sikhim; but an acre of Bass and Allsopp lay fermenting in the sun at Punkabarri, while no one seemed to have thought of the Sikhs, who were sickening for want of their indispensable "atta" (of the importance of which I was for the first time aware).

How we should have enjoyed the beer! but it is bulky, rapidly consumed, and its transport would make a great hole in a "Coolie Corps limited." What relief it would have been for the overworked transport in the plains if it had been left behind, or what quantities of rum, biscuit, and "atta" might have been sent up instead!

Five hundred rounds per man of ammunition for the 6th Royals alone had been ordered up, and the magazines at Darjeeling were small, damp, and already partly occupied.

Tents had also been sent up with the 6th Royals, and there were not half-a-dozen places in the whole country which we were about to enter where three ordinary bell-tents could have been pitched together.

I sent my Brigade-Major, Lieutenant Fryer, Rifle Brigade, to Punkabarri to arrange the stores, to point out those which were to be sent up, and to utilize some of the tents for the protection of other portions.

There is nothing which at some time or other may not be the business of the Commanding Officer if he wishes to assure himself of success.

Insufficiency of transport obliged me to be content with one column, and I selected as my point of crossing what is known as the site of the old Rungeet bridge, on the direct road to Namchi. An officer had been employed for some time here with a working party making a bridge across the Rungnoo (a small stream on our side of the Rungeet which intersects the road to the bridge).

The formation of the ground at the site selected for the bridge was most favourable for our purposes. A spur (on our side) approached the river at right angles, and then turned sharp to the left up the bank, until stopped by the Rungnoo; this latter part forming a parapet behind which a considerable force could be encamped, or works carried on, completely under cover from the enemy.

To the Hon. A. Eden, Special Commissioner.

SIR, DARJEELING, JAN. 26TH, 1861.

In answer to your letter, No. 5, of the 25th inst. . . . . . I have promised to inform you when I am prepared to move, and have even expressed my opinion as to the time, but I should fall short of my duty were I to start without previously informing you of any part of the organization whose efficiency I doubted.

I have *sufficient* transport, but its *quality* cannot be determined until it has been tested. The transport will *always* be more or less doubtful so long as we are dependent on coolies. Dr. Campbell is of opinion that they will be willing to accompany us to the Teesta, after which there are sufficient ponies.

To cross the Rungeet and drive the enemy from Namchi will be the best method of inspiring confidence, not only among the coolies, but throughout the population. Should the coolies, however, be unwilling to accompany us, I should recommend marching into the district lately occupied by Dr. Campbell. A short residence there would probably bring the whole coolie population belonging to it to our assistance.

To dislodge the enemy from Namchi is, however, as necessary, previous to taking the latter course, as it would be if we were about to march on Tumloong.

I have, &c.,

J. C. GAWLER,

Lieut.-Col., commanding Troops, Darjeeling.

To the Hon. A. Eden, Special Commissioner.

SIR, DARJEELING, JAN. 28TH, 1861.

In answer to your letter, No. 6, of the 26th inst. . . . . . For a small but sufficient force the transport is ample, without any speculation as to what assistance we are likely to receive in Sikhim. The Deputy Commissary-General's fears, as mentioned in para. 3 of your letter, were for the numbers with which I had furnished him (being the maximum which I wished to take in).

I apprehend no difficulty in taking ponies to Tumloong, as they have travelled in that country, and Dr. Hooker mentions having ridden from Tumloong to Darjeeling.

As regards the *quality*, I cannot approve of coolies as a means of transport, as they are liable to panics and to being tampered with, and I therefore on the 5th of this month urged the Commissariat to purchase or hire 400 ponies, which however were not procured, and previous to your arrival I endeavoured to obtain mules, by representing the state of the case to the Major-General commanding the division.

You were present yourself this morning when the coolies were mustered, and told that they were required for Sikhim, and you observed that they all appeared satisfied; still, I cannot feel that confidence in them that I should wish, and it was for this reason that I alluded, as mentioned in para. 5 of your letter, to the possibility of having to occupy the district lately occupied by Dr. Campbell, until coolies were ensured or other transport obtained.

The preparations have been unavoidably delayed, and although not complete within the seven days as I hoped, I trust that the expedition will be put in motion within the ten days mentioned by you.

I have, &c.,

J. C. Gawler,
Lieut.-Col.

To the Qr. Mast. General of the Army.

Sir, Darjeeling, Jan. 30th, 1861.

I have the honour to report for the information of His Excellency the Commander-in-Chief, that at the requisition, shortly after his arrival, of Mr. Eden, Envoy and Special Commissioner, I commenced preparations, which I have nearly completed, for an advance on Tumloong.

The want of transport prevents my moving a portion of my force, as I had desired, towards the country lately occupied by Dr. Campbell, and I am only able to take into the field about 600 men.

I endeavoured, on the 5th of this month, to obtain 400 ponies from the neighbouring districts, but only 93 have been procured, and some of them, I fear, are already non-effective.*

The Coolie Corps, numbering 420 (200 more expected on the 1st proximo), has been raised by the civil authority (Dr. Campbell), and by his advice and with the acquiescence of Major FitzGerald, Deputy Commissary-General, I have not removed the corps from civil control, but have appointed Lieutenant Becher, 73rd N.I., to the charge of it while in the field.

Provisions for five weeks, for the large force with which I had at first intended to move, will be completed at the old Rungeet bridge (our frontier), about the 1st of February.

Captain Impey, Field Engineer, who arrived about a week ago, commenced preparations at the Rungeet, by my desire, for a floating bridge, which is to be constructed in several pieces on our side of the river, and to be thrown across only when our supplies are completed and the force ready to advance; as to construct any other kind of bridge would necessitate the moving of a larger portion of the force down to the Rungeet, and the consequent employment on that service of considerable transport before the supplies are ready.

To carry out Captain Impey's requirements, I reinforced Lieutenant Beavan's party by a few Sikh police under Captain Baker.

We were allowed to collect a large quantity of material and to construct one portion of the bridge, and even to float it for trial, the enemy, as before, merely looking on; but the annexed reports from Captain Baker, commanding detachment of military police, will show that the enemy opened a heavy fire the following day, which stopped his working

* *Vide* pp. 21 and 64.

parties and wounded two men, in spite of some gabions which had been placed along the bank of the river by Captain Impey to protect them.

I went down in the evening, immediately on the receipt of Captain Baker's report, and observing that the enemy had got into a position from which the working parties at the river could not be defiladed, I ordered Captain Baker merely to cut and collect the material under cover (of which there is plenty, except on the edge of the river), and not to reply to the enemy's fire.

Distances are very deceptive, and heights which were supposed to be well out of shot, are ascertained on measurement to be only 500 yards.

The enemy have several jingalls and the rifles taken from the Sebundy Sappers.

I returned to Darjeeling on the morning of the 29th, and in communication with Mr. Eden and Major FitzGerald, have made arrangements for putting the force in motion.

The artillery go down to-day, and I intend moving the 6th Regiment down to-morrow.

I shall cross on Saturday the 2nd.

The bridge will be formed in a few hours, and I hope to move forward thence on Monday the 4th proximo.

Captain Dunbar, appointed to the charge of the Field Commissariat, unfortunately broke his collar-bone a few days after his arrival. On the requisition of Major FitzGerald, Deputy Commissary-General, I have placed at his disposal the services of Captain Cafe, V.C., temporarily commanding the wing, 73rd N.I., for employment as Field Commissariat Officer, he being the only available officer, and of considerable experience.

I have, &c.,

JOHN C. GAWLER,

Lieut.-Colonel, commanding Sikhim Field Force.

CHAPTER III.

Instructions regarding baggage and equipment—advantage of the first blow—principles of warfare in a difficult country—marching through a pass—3rd February, passage of the Rungeet—night march—four men wounded — 9th February, difficult ascent — concealed breastworks — European wounded — Namchi — designs of the enemy — night march to turn position of Sandoopchi — waylay the enemy — Major Maitland — transport — smooth-bore and rifle in cover shooting — night marches — 20th February, arrangements at Namchi — three columns towards the Teesta — Captain Impey's march — surprises the enemy — Lassoo Kajee—at what point to cross Teesta—reasons for cutting bridges—position of Neh and bridge—supplies and transport—coolies or ponies—night reconnaissance—prisoners and 3-pr. gun surrendered by the enemy —28th February, Radoong Ghât—seize the bridge—Neh—booby traps —reconnaissance—new style of bridge—more prisoners surrendered—preparations for advance on Tumloong.

Before advancing into the enemy's country I consulted with commanding officers, and gave instructions regarding baggage and equipment ;—

Native establishments of the European troops were to be left behind.

As we should bivouac, and there would be plenty of firewood, the men would form their own knots at their own fires, with due regard to their squads. Hence, every man would carry his own cooking utensils, which were to consist of a drinking-tin and a tin with a lid for cooking coffee. (Meat done on the coals is far more suitable in the field, though the coffee-tin would be available for any who did not think so.)

The men were to carry two blankets. Great coats, as it would be dry weather, and as not being so useful for sleeping in, were to be left behind. On sentry, a blanket to be worn over the shoulders, doubled over a string round the neck.

Each man was to carry a second pair of boots, some soap, and any small article that might be approved by the Commanding Officer.

Forage caps were to be worn. (Owing to a misconception, helmets were also brought; but these disappeared in the jungles within the first three days.)

The men were to be allowed to sew their blankets together lengthways, and to make eyelet-holes in the lower edges, and to be advised to do this in knots of three. Two uprights and a ridge-pole could be found at any halting-place, and this patrol tent stretched over it. One end would be closed up with bushes, or with a piece of sacking, spare blanket, or other material sewn on. Three men then get inside with four blankets.*

Officers were limited to one coolie, but were recommended to use a pack-pony instead, which a soldier would be allowed to lead. Not many followed this advice; first, because it was positively asserted by many acquainted with the country that it was impracticable for horses; second, because no one had a pack-saddle like mine.

* My own tent was the ordinary blanket patrol tent, used during the Kaffir War. The blankets were large enough to allow a wall 18 inches high. Braid sewn across in the direction of the strain of the cords, will prevent the blanket tearing. In wet weather, or when dews are heavy, this tent requires an outer fly of calico or ticken, otherwise it retains a large quantity of water, is of an enormous weight, and on being rolled up soaks everything through with which it comes in contact.

Nearly all these arrangements were those which, during three years of a Kaffir War, experienced commanding officers had, after various trials, adopted as those which worked best and gave most satisfaction. There is so much in the service that is necessarily done by rule, word of command, and according to pattern, that it is a real relief to the soldier when any rules can be relaxed, and it makes him think that he has actually some time to himself when he is allowed to light his own fire and do his own bit of beef on the coals. This latter, however, is only practicable when there is an abundance of fuel in proportion to the force.

The next point to be studied was the coolie loads:—

The howitzers (12-pounders) required eight coolies each.

Carriages for ditto, say ten each.

Ammunition would be carried in boxes on the few mules that were available.

Biscuit was in tins of 100 lbs., rather heavy for a *travelling* load for a hill coolie, and therefore one tin was generally assigned to two of them, or to four Dhanga coolies (though the latter were not present at the outset).

Rice in sacks, either for two hill coolies or four Dhangas.

Rum, in casks, I think also required two hill coolies or four Dhangas. I suppose the casks were 18 gallons.

It has been already mentioned that the point selected for crossing the Rungeet was near the site of the old bridge, and that the ground admitted of a considerable force being encamped near the river completely covered from the enemy by a sharp spur. On this spur a place was prepared for the guns facing the stockades, where they would be quite concealed until required.

In dealing with an uncivilized enemy it is a great point to begin, if possible, with a severe lesson, and, having gained their respect, to provide them such ample occupation of taking care of themselves, as will allow them no time for offensive enterprises: in other words, to force them on the defensive and keep them there. It saves an incalculable amount of trouble, expense, and bloodshed.

It was with these views that I was anxious not to

frighten the enemy by the sight of the guns, or by any firing, until I was quite ready, when, if they were determined to try their strength, they would receive such a lesson as would render them indisposed to molest us during our difficult march. I dreaded an attack upon our timid coolies, a couple of shots among whom might have deprived us of the whole of our transport.

The character of this kind of warfare, when there are great difficulties of country *as well as* the enemy to contend with, is to advance well-supplied camps step by step, improving the communications towards the object to be attained, and to patrol from them in light marching order. The object of course would be some capital, stronghold, or other base which even the nomad must possess. In moving the camps, the best and most direct road should be left for the baggage, and all the bye-roads and paths filled with parties exploring by different routes towards the next camp. Thus a force may always maintain the offensive without harassing the troops. If there be a difficult locality or district, of which the enemy is fond, whence he makes his raids, or which he uses as a hiding place, *that* is the spot wherein to form a camp, and lay open with roads until the spell is broken.

In the Kaffir War, *beyond a day or two's march from a town or post*, "trekking" round the country, *escorting as it were our own baggage and supplies*, did little good. It was labour and risk for the troops, and rather furnished the enemy with amusement. Nothing was thoroughly effectual, until we formed camps *in* the enemy's strongholds, and patrolled thence and opened the communications.

The British soldier can force his way *wherever he can be fed*, but you cannot carry on offensive operations, and perform escort duty, with the same body of troops at one and the same time.

In a mountainous, densely wooded, or difficult country, it will often happen that the route lies through a pass, ravine, or forest, where it is impossible to crown heights, or to use flank patrols, without making an operation of it, for which there is neither the time nor the force to spare. The best method of procedure then is, without checking the advance, to drop one or more files from the head of the column (at suitable distances in mere jungle, or in other cases at well-selected points as they are reached), to watch the heights, jungle, or other places likely to favour an enemy. The column or convoy thus moves forward under the constant protection of halted and well-posted sentries. Sections may be dropped at suitable distances and places as supports. When the tail of the column has passed about 200 yards, the files which have been dropped follow in succession, gradually rejoining the column by sections or companies. A regiment or brigade may thus move any distance by jungle paths, or among rocks, by constant inversion in perfect safety. It is on the principles of the rules which were formerly laid down for street firing, but which appear to have been expunged from the Field Exercises.

For the protection of camps, the curtain or semicircular screen of sentries adopted by large armies in regular warfare is insufficient in dealing with an uncivilized enemy; first, because your camps are comparatively very small and more easily turned; secondly, because the enemy has no tactical rear; a cordon of sentries completely encircling the camp is absolutely necessary. Against such foes, however, though redoubled precision, subtlety, and vigilance are necessary, the arrangements happily need not be of so formidable a character; and an occasional counterplot or judicious ambuscade will do more to secure the repose and safety of the camp than doubling all the outposts.

To the Qr. Mast. General of the Army.

SIR, CAMP, GREAT RUNGEET, FEB. 3RD, 1861.

I have the honour to report, in continuation of my letter of the 30th ultimo, that the Royal Artillery marched on Thursday, so as to get by night into the position which had been selected for them, and which commanded the site of our intended bridge and the enemy's stockades.

Two hundred and fifty-three men of the 1st and 3rd Battalions of Military Police had been encamped for some time under cover near the site of the proposed bridge, together with a working party of Sebundy Sappers, under Lieut. Beavan, and a guard of the 73rd N.I., with a view partially of enticing the enemy to collect to oppose our passage.

Material had been collected in abundance by the Sebundy Sappers, and I had requested Captain Impey, Field Engineer, to prepare a bridge that could be quickly put together and thrown across, and that during Friday he should make as much display in preparations for crossing as could be made without exposing the men.

I directed one wing of H.M. 6th Regiment, with the whole of the field baggage, to encamp near the site of the proposed bridge.

The execution of these operations at the bridge I confided to Major Maitland, 79th Highlanders, acquainting him with my own intended movements, and directing him to shell the enemy's camp and stockades, and prepare the bridge, under a covering party on Saturday morning; but not to cross until my appearance unless he could do so without risking a single man.

In the meantime Captain Murray, at my request, proceeded to the Upper Rungeet Guard on Thursday evening; and at night, with fifty Sebundy Sappers, marched to a concealed spot about two miles up the river, upon which we had previously agreed, where I had told him to construct a raft in the jungle with all secrecy.

Four companies of H.M. 6th Regiment left Sinchul on Thursday about noon, carrying three days' provisions and one blanket per man. I joined at Darjeeling, and took them down the Goke road, on the Tugwar Spur, and halted halfway down at about 5 o'clock, until dusk, when I moved on and took a path to the right leading down to the Rungeet, which I reached at 1½ on Friday morning. I left them there all day concealed in the jungle, and enjoining silence and directing that no one should quit the camp, proceeded myself to the Upper Rungeet Guard, to ascertain that all was ready and to give further instructions, and returned in the evening At dusk I took them through the jungles to the rendezvous agreed on with Captain Murray. On the way there I lost the road for some hours, and although we slid down almost a precipice, and had to force and cut our way through the dense jungle on a dark night, our difficulties only elicited merriment. We reached the appointed spot at about 1 A.M. on Saturday, and had to get the raft out of the jungle and float it. A Sebundy Sapper then went across with a pliant cane, but it was with considerable difficulty (Captain Murray himself working above his waist in water) that the raft was put in order, and sixteen sappers landed on the other side. It was not till about 7½ A.M. that two companies of H.M. 6th Regiment had been ferried over; and, as Major Maitland's signal guns had fired, I moved on up the hill towards the head of the mountain path, directing Captain Unwin, when the remaining companies should have crossed, to go round by the bank of the river to take the stockades in flank should they not be already vacated, or in case I should be delayed in coming down the hill.

All this was performed with great spirit, and entirely to my satisfaction; but on my coming down from above the stockades, I found the enemy had fled, and we could only see four or five in the distance making the best of their way off.*

My best thanks are due to Major Maitland for the promptness and skill with which he executed the work assigned to him; (I annex his report, and fully concur in the praise he has bestowed on Captain Impey, R.E., for his skill and energy in making the bridge and throwing it across;†)—

* This was not bad as a first attempt at a night march, which is always a difficult undertaking; but we ought to have reached the raft at 9 P.M. instead of 1 A.M.; and we should then have reached the top of the hill by daylight, instead of having only crossed the river at 7.30 A.M. We managed several after this perfectly.

† I regret that I have not a copy of this report. Captain Impey's bridge was a complete success, and the throwing it across was effected under Captain Impey's personal directions, under a smart fire from the enemy's stockades, notwithstanding that the bank was lined with our skirmishers, and that the howitzers from the spur plied the stockades. Four of Baker's Sikhs were wounded. For description of this bridge, *vide* paras. 6–10, Captain Impey's Report, p. 92.

to Captain Baker, Lieut. Gouldsbury, and the officers and men of the 1st and 3rd Battalions Military Police, who for several days had worked with a right good will, collecting materials and carrying out the arrangements for crossing; to Lieut. Heathcote, Deputy Assistant Quartermaster-General, for carrying out correctly all my arrangements, collecting the materials and troops at the appointed stations; to Lieut. Fryer, R.B., officiating Brigade-Major, who has, since my taking command, rendered me every assistance, and who accompanied me with the wings of the 6th Regiment; and to Captain Murray, commanding Sebundy Sappers, whose services I have already alluded to; and I beg to assure His Excellency that with a force in which such unity and energy are combined, no insurmountable difficulty will present itself.

I have, &c.,

JOHN C. GAWLER, Lieut.-Colonel,
Commanding Sikhim Field Force.

To the Qr. Mast. General of the Army.

SIR, CAMP NEAR NAMCHI, FEB. 9TH, 1861.

I have the honour, in continuation of my last, to report my further operations for the information of His Excellency the Commander-in-Chief.

Royal Artillery	36
2 12-pounder howitzers	
6th Regiment	320
73rd N.I.	—
1st & 3rd Military Police	253
Sebundy Sappers	100

I had collected near the Rungeet bridge, after the passage had been effected, force as per margin, and on Monday, the 4th instant, I proceeded with Baker's Sikhs to a spring of water within a mile of Mikh, with the double object of reconnoitring and securing the top of the hill before I moved any baggage.

On the face of the hill, and about half-way up, opposite our bridge, was a small spring, where I directed a company of H.M. 6th Regiment to be posted, and where about 100 or 200 of the enemy had been encamped.

Between the top of the hill and Mikh are three springs, in the neighbourhood of which not less than 2000 of the enemy, it is said, have been encamped within the last four or five days.

I directed Captain Baker to encamp at the second spring, and the piquets were being posted, when two jingalls and three musket shots were fired about four miles in advance, apparently as a signal, and some voices were heard in the neighbourhood. I took a party of thirty men, and with Captain Baker proceeded to reconnoitre. No one was to be seen, but apparently seven men had retired before us. We went to Mikh, about a mile and a half farther on, and then made a circuit to our left to the top of Sillok Voke Ridge, and returned to Captain Baker's camp, whence I and my staff returned to the Rungeet.

On the following morning, the 5th instant, leaving Major Maitland in command of the Rungeet, with orders that the sappers should improve the road, and that the artillery, baggage, and stores should be moved up the hill to Mikh,* I took two companies H.M. 6th along the ridge on the left of the road, and proceeded to the top of Sillok Voke; thence I sent one company, which was encumbered with its blankets, direct into camp, while Captain Unwin, H.M. 6th Foot, Captain Murray, Sebundy Sappers, and Lieut.

* "The march here was most difficult, through dense forests, along a mere "footpath hanging over the khud, only a foot or a foot and a half broad "in many places, with an ascent of one in four to one in six. By many "acquainted with the country it was believed that the force could not have "come up without the greatest difficulty. . . . In addition to the march up "the heights, the Europeans made a long detour with Colonel Gawler, from "which they have only just returned. . . . I regret to say that during this "detour, Colonel Gawler got amongst some of the enemy's stockades near this "camp, and one European received two bullets in the leg."—*Hon. A. Eden to Secretary to Government Bengal, dated Camp Mikh, 5th Feb.*, 1861.

Fryer, R.B., officiating Brigade-Major, accompanied me with the other one along a more northerly spur, which would bring us into the Namchi road, about two miles below and beyond our camp at Mikh. On descending the spur, we observed a fire burning, beyond the junction of the roads, on a narrow neck which connects Sillok Voke Hill with the Namchi plateau. Moving rapidly forward, the flanking parties caught momentary sight of some of the enemy in the jungles, and the advanced files, under Lieut. Delafosse, received a volley by which Private Arkison, H.M. 6th Regiment, had his thigh broken. A charge of about 50 yards upon the enemy discovered to us that we had carried several well-constructed breastworks. Leaving a few files with the wounded man, we followed the enemy for about half a mile, and then returned (as it was late in the afternoon), inspected and destroyed the breastworks, made a stretcher for the wounded man, and went back to camp by the road, which it had been our object to explore.

The breastworks, about six in number, were of stone, on the right and left of the road, rather oblique to it, and in echellon with each other. The upper one was about 12 feet long, 5 feet high in front, almost 2 feet thick at the top, and covered with grass and fern thrown lightly against it, by which it was thoroughly concealed. When leaving, we heard about fifty shots near Namchi, a great deal of shouting, and saw a dense smoke.

It had not been my intention to leave Mikh for two or three days, until all the stores, &c., had been pushed up; but, under the circumstances of my having come into collision with the enemy when reconnoitring in advance of my camp, I considered it proper to advance upon Namchi on the next day, the 6th instant.

We reached Namchi without molestation; but on our encamping, three signal guns were fired from the steep ascent leading to Sandoopchi. We found the large house,

E. Stanford, Charing Cross

THREE MILES OF THIS TO SANDOOPCHI,
WITH "BOOBY TRAP".

or gumpa, belonging to Lassoo Kajee, the head man of this district, burned down and still smouldering, which accounted for the smoke of the previous day. Some supposed it to have been done by the enemy, because Lassoo Kajee was favourably disposed towards us, and others believe it to have been by his own orders. It was a large and good house, with walls of rammed earth, 54 feet × 48 feet.

In the afternoon I learned from Mr. Eden that there were 400 men under the Dewan's brother at Sandoopchi, about three miles above us, the ascent to which is by a very narrow and almost perpendicular ridge, and that it was their intention when we arrived at Namchi to make a flank march by Cheadam, and double into our territory by the Rungeet, at our own bridge.* Against this I had provided by having left a strong guard of two howitzers and some of Renny's Sikhs and 73rd N.I. at the bridge, and by having ordered Major Maitland to proceed on the 7th instant with two companies H.M. 6th Regiment and 100 Ghoorka Police *viâ* Cheadam to Namchi.

Though the enemy had shown a disinclination for a direct encounter, it seemed to me that men ought not to be risked against such a position as Sandoopchi if there were any possibility of turning it. I therefore called suddenly on the night of the 6th for a few volunteers, whom I readily found in Captain Murray, commanding Sebundy Sappers, Lieut. Heathcote, D.A.Q.M.G., Lieut. Fryer, R.B., officiating Brigade-Major, Lieut. Roberts, and 3 men, R.A.; Lieut. Wilson and 14 men H.M. 6th Regiment; Captain Baker, Lieut. Wanchope, Mr. Garstin, Lieut. Hidyat Alli, and 34 men 1st Battalion Military Police; Lieut. Rice, Lieut. Delafosse, and Dr. Hodgson, R.A.

I directed the guide to lead us to a point on the main ridge running south from Mount Tendong, whence I had

* *Vide* p. 43.

previously noticed there was a comparatively easy ascent nearly to the top of the mountain, and to about two miles above and in rear of Sandoopchi.

We started at about 9½ P.M., and I left directions with Captain Unwin, commanding wing H.M. 6th Regiment, to move an hour before daylight direct up to Sandoopchi. The night was very dark, the jungle dense, and path rugged; but about 7 A.M., by steady marching, we had gained the position above Sandoopchi. To enable the men to recover their breath, as the last ascent had been very steep, I halted the party in the jungle, nearly parallel with, and about 10 to 15 paces from the wide, well-beaten path from Namchi to the Teesta. The last man was not up, when voices were heard of people coming up the road from Sandoopchi, and presently the head of a party, marching two deep, with sloped arms, turned a corner about 50 yards from us, approaching the tree behind which I stood at the edge of the path, and marching unsuspectingly across the front of my party. About sixty had come in sight (they were tall men with iron helmets, and their gun-barrels very long and bright), when the guide, who had been only listening, suddenly caught sight of their guns, and sprang deeper into the jungle. In another moment they would have been close up to me; but they suddenly paused, turned, and dashed down a steep "khud" to their left. As they turned we fired and charged, but no bodies were left in the road; eagerness carried many of our party through the dense jungle and down the "khud" farther than they would have gone had they reflected that they would have to get back again.*

* I submit this account for the consideration of musketry instructors. The 6th Regiment had the highest figure of merit for that year in Bengal. The arm of precision was at a disadvantage. Brown Bess, with half-a-dozen "loopers" on the top of the bullet, was most deadly in waylaying at the Cape during the Kaffir War.

To philanthropists I must offer the following explanation: As I stood, a little in advance of the right of my party, looking down the path at the

We continued down to Sandoopchi, searching both sides of the road, and all along saw traces of precipitate flight of large numbers through the jungles to our left, *i.e.* in the direction of the Cheadam road. At Sandoopchi we met Captain Unwin, with one company H.M. 6th Regiment, and found the enemy's cantonments, which apparently had been vacated about daylight. There were numerous large well-built comfortable huts, with raised sleeping places, a shed also for cattle and horses; and odds and ends were left in confusion. A path showed that a large party had gone more deliberately through the jungles to the Cheadam road, which convinced me that this force was retiring* in two bodies, one *viâ* Cheadam towards Bhotan or Dikkeeling, and the one I had surprised towards Tumloong. The former, we hear from the Cheadam people, have retreated hastily and terrified across the Teesta; but I much regret I did not order Captain Unwin to pursue them by their path through the jungle, and send two fresh companies in support; the operations would have been more complete.

We reached our camp at Namchi at 9 A.M. on the 7th.

The roads in our front and rear are being improved and remade by Captain Impey.

Major Maitland joined me on the 8th; I enclose his report. I propose sending him from this round about the junction of the Rungeet and Rumaam rivers *viâ* Seriong to Goke;

---

enemy marching towards me two-deep across the front of my party, and within from 10 to 15 paces of the muzzles of their rifles, I said to myself, "This is murder!" and whispered to Captain Murray to tell the guide to step out and call upon them to lay down their arms. As they turned and dashed off, however, I admit, seeing that they were eluding my grasp, to having shouted the command, "blaze away"; not that it affected the matter at all, for the volley if anything was before the command.

* It seems quite as probable that these parties, being on the only two practicable routes to Cheadam, were proceeding *thither* to carry out their intentions of assailing our communications. (See p. 41.)

whence I intend he shall operate towards Rinchingpoong and Pemionchi, if the transport can be obtained; this will enable Lieut. Pierson, R.E., to open that district with roads and bridges.

Transport is still a great drawback; the coolies of the country present an irritating mixture of indolence, timidity, and independence. The country is quite practicable for mules.

We have no sickness.

I am much indebted to Mr. Eden, who has kindly undertaken the Intelligence Department, for which his tact in managing the natives, and his way of reasoning with them, render him particularly fit.

I have, &c.,

JOHN C. GAWLER, Lieut.-Colonel,
Commanding Sikhim Expedition.

This seems a suitable place to say a word about arms. The great value of the Enfield rifle is its long range, and non-military readers must not confound a rifle simple with a breech-loader. At short ranges, say 80 yards and under, the chances of hitting are in favour of the larger bored musket or carbine. The latter is specially adapted for snap shots and close work, and so well was this understood in the Kaffir War by the rebel Hottentots, who are crack shots, that they used to cut down to carbine length the muskets they deserted with or captured, and would then fit them with bone fore-sights.

With the large smooth bore, moreover, it is practicable to use, either with or without the bullet, six or eight "loopers" or slugs, which act like small canister at upwards of 100 yards, and are very useful if you get into unpleasant company at short ranges. I imagine the double-barrelled carbine and a few old Brunswick rifles with the sword-bayonet would prove far more serviceable among our native levies in Ashantee than the Enfield; for it seems very questionable whether Ashantees will be caught in the open. A proportion of Enfields might be entrusted to picked men.

Night marches, which are of immense value when well performed, require the greatest patience and attention in their execution. During the Kaffir War we frequently made them, with variable success. Their failure was generally attributable to want of patience. On a wagon road matters are tolerably easy, but when it comes to footpaths over rough ground, or through bush, where it is pitch dark in addition, it is trying in the extreme. There should be a first-rate officer in rear, and the head of the column should halt as a rule every ten minutes or quarter of an hour, according to the ground, to allow the rear to close up.

A mile an hour is the utmost that should be counted on by footpaths.

In the night march to Sandoopchi we were very successful. The path for the first four miles might be termed "dreadful," even by daylight. I knew that there was no precipice or place where a man could injure himself, and was therefore unable to refrain from transgressing my own orders as to strict silence, and going into fits of laughter, as an occasional crash told that one of our party had come to grief, and a cry of terror divulged that he was quite unaware whether he was falling 5 feet or 500. Europeans indulged in laughter a little too loud for the secrecy of the occasion whenever they found that no harm was done, but Sikhs would not smile until day broke. I halted for upwards of an hour and a half to rest the men as soon as I reached the spur leading up to Mount Tendong, under the impression that there was a path, but when the guide came to explain himself, and we came to try it, we found that there was no path, though comparatively open jungle and a tolerably smooth ascent.

From a military point of view the delay rendered the enterprise imperfect, as otherwise we should have caught the enemy in his camp before he was moving, instead of only falling in with his advanced guard. On the other hand, the effect produced proved ample, and it is gratifying therefore to have achieved it without the loss of life that would certainly have resulted.

To the Qr. Mast. General of the Army.

CAMP, RUNGPODAN, ON TEESTA RIVER, SIKHIM,
FEB. 20TH, 1861.

SIR,

I have the honour to report that, on the 14th inst., I had assembled one company H.M. 6th Regiment, 100 Baker's Sikhs, Detachment Royal Artillery with two 12-pounder howitzers and rockets, Sebundy Sappers, and supplies at Buckcheem, a spring of water near the top of Mount Tendong, and about five hours' march from Namchi. I had also two companies H.M. 6th Regiment at Sandoopchi, about two miles lower down in our rear.

I left one company H.M. 6th Regiment and 70 Ghoorka Police at Namchi, in charge of stores and for escort and patrolling purposes.

Before leaving Namchi, Captain Impey, Field Engineer, at my desire constructed a rough block-house and commissariat store, and cleared the jungle to a good distance round, as it will be my main depôt in advance of the Great Rungeet.

I acquainted Major Maitland, H.M. 79th Highlanders, commanding Convalescent Depôt, with my general plan of operations, and with the state of the commissariat and transport, and entrusted him with the command from Darjeeling to Namchi.

1. Arrangements being completed, I ordered one company H.M. 6th Regiment, under Capt. Unwin, from Sandoopchi, to meet 40 Ghoorkas from Namchi on the afternoon of the 14th inst., at a point on the main range, nearly three miles S. of Mount Tendong, and to proceed thence and encamp at Nunderoom, moving next day *viâ* Purveem and Burmiok to Temi.

2. Captain Impey, Bengal Engineers, was to quit San-

doopchi, with one company H.M. 6th Regiment, at daylight on the 15th inst.; pick up the artillery, 40 Baker's Sikhs, Sebundy Sappers, and supplies, at Buckcheem, and proceed over Mount Tendong direct to Temi.

3. With one company H.M. 6th Regiment, under Captain Kendall, 60 Baker's Sikhs, 4 gunners with rockets, under Lieut. Roberts, commanding R.A., and 20 Sebundy Sappers, I quitted Buckcheem at daylight on the 15th inst., and proceeded along the main ridge in a northerly direction from Mount Tendong, with the intention of coming down on the monastery of Neongong, and so threatening the communications of the enemy, and compelling them either to fight at one or all of these places, or to retire across the Teesta, as they were reported to be at Neongong, Nampoke, Neh, Temi, and Bermiok.

The right column, through a mistake of the officer with the Ghoorkas, did not reach Temi by the route named, but their showing themselves in that part of the country tolerably fulfilled the object, as the enemy disappeared.

With the left column I traversed the main range by an old path not recently used, until 4 P.M.; and as we found no water, and the range took a wider westerly sweep than represented in the map, I was compelled to turn down the spur next to that on which Neongong is situated, to ensure finding water before being benighted.

Half-way down, *i.e.* about 3¼ miles above the Teesta, at about 5½ P.M., we debouched from the jungle upon some villages, below which a "tom tom" was sounding. I halted the men to ascertain the cause, and observed that nearly all the villagers were on the move towards the river, except one family in a house near us, which I immediately surrounded, and sent the guide forward to interrogate the owner, who was an old man and the only male in the house. There were several women and children; they appeared curious, but not in the least alarmed.

I learned from this man, that it had become known the day before that our force had left Namchi, and therefore all the villagers were ordered by their Lamas to cross the Teesta, but that he had determined on staying; that the English had been expected that day at Temi, and therefore 100 warriors, under Kabee Kajee, had gone there from Neh to fight them; that Neongong was deserted, and that nearly all the fighting men had crossed the Teesta, and that there were bridges at Bhomsong, Neh, Linsing, and Took; that about a quarter of an hour before we arrived four men had left him, who had come from Kabee Kajee's party *en route* to Temi, to ask him if there were any signs of troops, as they wished to have all clear in rear; that he was to keep a sharp look-out, as troops often appeared unexpectedly.

As it was nearly dusk, and we had been marching since daylight without water, I was compelled to encamp, otherwise I should have wished to have waylaid the road by which the 100 warriors would return to Neh. (These men were surprised by the centre column under Captain Impey,* whose report I annex.)

* I have no copy of this report, and as Captain Impey alludes to it very slightly in his final report, I here give Mr. Eden's account of it:—

No. 14. 17th February, 1861. To the Secretary to Government.

Para. 3. "We marched for nearly twelve hours, cutting a road for the "artillery as we came: we passed over the conical summit of Mount Tendong, "8663 feet; snow was laying on the top of this mountain, and it was most "difficult and dangerous work getting the guns and baggage down the abrupt "and slippery descent of the hill to this place (Temi), which is situated in "the Teesta valley, at an elevation of 4790 feet. The artillery did not get "into camp until 11½ P.M.

4. "On arriving at Temi we took the enemy's camp entirely by surprise, "and got amongst them while they were eating their dinner, their outlying "pickets having apparently just been withdrawn. A volley was poured into "them, and they were followed by skirmishers for about two miles, a running "fire being kept up the whole way. They threw away their clothes and "weapons, and made off into the jungle towards the Teesta."

I considered it expedient that our point for crossing the Teesta should be within, at most, three days' march of Tumloong (to obviate our being obliged to form any large depôts on the other side of the river); but, as this would necessitate a march for some distance up the right bank from Temi, I determined on cutting all bridges below the point I might select, so that neither my force nor convoys might be liable to annoyance during what would be a flank march.

I therefore started the next morning, an hour before daylight, to search for bridges, and about nine o'clock found a large one at the Linsing Ghât, a few miles above the Took Ghât. On approaching it I was met by three natives bearing a flag of truce and two letters, which were immediately forwarded to Mr. Eden, the Special Commissioner.

The natives informed me that Lassoo Kajee was on the other side and wished to come across.

As I knew that Mr. Eden wished every facility to be afforded to natives to come in and return to their villages, and had heard Lassoo Kajee's name mentioned particularly, I said that he might come, and concealed my men in the jungles along the bank, near the bridge. There were several hours' delay while he was getting (as they informed us) his baggage ready, and during this time we observed that the stockades opposite were full of men, armed with matchlocks and rifles; I also observed one or two jingalls. Across the river was about a stone's throw, and the opposite jungle was thick with faces peeping at us. There was a strongly marked difference between these curious ones and those who manned the stockades. The tall figures, features, attitudes, and demeanours of the latter were totally unlike the effeminate Lepcha, or even the Bhooteas whom I have hitherto seen. I was informed that they were Thibeteans, the guard of the Sikhim Rajah, who had sent a detachment of them to every bridge.

As Mr. Eden had told me that he did not wish me to stop

operations for anything, I informed Lassoo Kajee when he arrived that I had come to cut the bridge. He replied that he had given orders that no one should cross while he was negotiating, but I told him that I could not spare a picket to see that his orders were not disobeyed, nor did I want to have to make a second trip, and that if he wished to recross at that point he could do so on a raft. (Rafts do not take long in making, but require five men, at least, on each side to work them, and will only take from fifteen to twenty men at a time. A party crossing to annoy us would not be satisfied with a raft as a means of retreat. By a hot pursuit they might all be caught, for the men would not stop to work the raft.)

Lassoo Kajee at length said that his own men should destroy the stockades and the bridge, and after some more time spent in parleying, and the guards removing their baggage and marching out, this was effected.*

We then left, and Lassoo Kajee accompanied us, and asked us to send an escort with him to Mr. Eden at Temi, for he was on his way there on the previous evening, and hearing firing ran down again, and falling on the rocks hurt his leg severely. Ascending the ridge towards our camp we saw Mr. Eden and Cheboo Lama coming down the ridge behind us from Temi, he having understood that I was encamped on the river bank. I returned to him with Lassoo Kajee, and

* "On leaving Namchi, the force was divided into three parties, the main "column, under Captain Impey, proceeding direct towards the Teesta, and "two parties, under Colonel Gawler and Captain Unwin respectively, making "long detours to the left and right, with the view of all reuniting again at "the Teesta. Captain Impey's column surprised the Sikhimese camp at "Temi; they fled, leaving their clothes and weapons, and were pursued down "within a few miles of the Teesta. From that time no further attempt at "opposition was made: the people were perfectly paralysed at the rapid "movements of the troops, whom they perceived to be advancing in several "directions at once, by forced marches, through dense forests, and over "pathless mountains, traversing in one day distances which even the natives "of these hills considered to be three fair marches."—*Extract from Mr. Eden's final report*, *No.* 40, *April 8th*, 1861.

we then went to the river bank and talked with some of the people on the opposite side, and it was arranged that those who wished might cross on rafts. Mr. Eden then returned to Temi and I to my camp.

On the next day I shifted camp to this place, and on the 18th instant, leaving my camp standing, I patrolled to Neongong, which I found deserted. I reconnoitred towards Neh and returned to camp, where, in the meantime, Mr. Eden and Captain Impey, with the guns, had arrived. The Sebundy Sappers have improved the road from Temi to this place. It was very steep and almost impassable for horses, although all came down before it was altered.

Yesterday I went with Captain Impey for two or three miles to examine the road towards Neh, and to reconnoitre. The road from this place to Bhomsong Ghât leads over Neh, which is an elevated "maidan," above the Teesta, at the termination of a spur with steep and rocky sides. The path is commanded by stone and bamboo breastworks, and there is a sort of stone fort at the top. It was here that the Ghoorkas were repulsed in 1789. Below Neh is a bridge guarded by stockades, and the enemy continue on the alert, marching down and filling the stockades as soon as the signal fire bursts up or the signal shot is heard.

As there is a good road, and it is but two or three days' march from this bridge to Tumloong, I have some idea of seizing it and Neh, and making it my crossing place instead of Bhomsong, as I had originally intended. Mr. Eden, however, wishes me to delay a few days to encourage all who are well disposed to come over, and he hopes also that the British subjects who are prisoners with the enemy will be given up.

SUPPLIES AND TRANSPORT.—I have more than a fortnight's provisions here, and there are more than another fortnight's at the Rungeet.

My Commissariat and Transport give me considerable trouble and anxiety. The difficulties of the Commissariat Department are much increased by the bad Transport. It is now apparent to everyone that the hill coolies on monthly wages are not fit material for a transport corps. Starting with their loads they take their own time, and deliver them at their own convenience. They have no caste, and stores frequently diminish alarmingly during their transit. The approaching rains, and amount of work that had to be done beforehand, rendered it inexpedient to delay operations until they should be further reorganized, and it is very doubtful whether, with their indolence and independence, those enlisted would not have run away rather than submit to discipline. At the present time this is troublesome and annoying, but may be profitable experience for the future. Hill coolies, I think, should only be employed "ticca," at so much per maund for a certain distance, and paid on delivery. I had some time before inquired about coolies from the plains, but had been told that they would not serve or suit, and it was only after the arrival of Mr. Eden, who procured seventy-six Dhanga coolies, that I learned their value. Two Dhanga coolies carry between them a little more than one hill coolie will carry, but they go quicker, are honest, and easily controlled, and it is of them I should reorganize a coolie corps should it be necessary to maintain one.*

In the meantime I must again urge mules or hill ponies as the proper description of transport to accompany a column in this country. Two Dhangas or one hill coolie carry, say one maund (80 lbs.), or about one soldier's rations for one month, but the coolies themselves require one seer (2 lbs.) per diem each man, while a mule or pony will live luxuriously on bamboo.†

* *Vide* p. 64.

† At Darjeeling and in these hills there is no grass, or at any rate only a few patches, and those generally *imported*. Horses are fed on bamboo leaves, and fatten on them.

From the officers of my staff I have received every assistance, and the whole force continues to perform cheerfully and to their utmost all that I require of them.

I have, &c.,

J. C. GAWLER, Lieut.-Colonel,
Commanding Sikhim Field Force.

P.S.—Accompanied by the officers of my staff, Lieut. Roberts, commanding Royal Artillery, and two or three others, I went the night before last through the jungle, to inspect the bridge below Neh, and to choose a place for the guns, in the event of its being necessary to seize it.

We made our reconnaissance and returned at 2 A.M. Yesterday two of the prisoners, *viz.* the Moonshee and Baboo, were given up, and the 3-pr. gun was brought to the river bank. They are making a raft for it, and it will be brought in to-day.

To the Qr. Mast. General of the Army.

CAMP, RADOONG GHÂT, TEESTA RIVER, SIKHIM,
FEB. 28TH, 1861.

SIR,

In my last from Camp Rungpodan of the 20th inst. I reported having discontinued operations at the request of the Special Commissioner, during which interval two prisoners and the 3-pr. gun were given up.

I have now the honour to report that, having decided on this Ghât as my point for crossing the river Teesta, I made arrangements for a move at Mr. Eden's further request, and started at midnight on the 24th inst. with 30 men H.M. 6th Regiment, 60 Baker's Sikhs, and 30 Royal Artillery, with two 12-pr. howitzers, with the view of getting into position before daylight to prevent the enemy cutting the cane bridge, which would be of the greatest assistance to us in the construction of our own.

I was requested by Mr. Eden not to cross or commence hostilities unless the enemy fired on us first, or attempted to cut away the bridge.

I reached the ground at about 3 A.M., and lined the bank of the river with skirmishers well concealed. The guns which had been carried by Dhanga coolies were mounted and placed in position, commanding the stockades and small open maidan in their rear. The enemy's watch-fires were burning in all the stockades.

I had a few nights previously ascertained that the enemy kept no picket on our side of the river. Had the contrary been the case I should have kept the force concealed as near as I could approach until daylight, and should then have rushed upon the picket and occupied the bank of the river to prevent those on the other side cutting the bridge.

It was half an hour before daylight before we were observed, and after the enemy had recovered from a momentary astonishment, two men made signs that they wished to cross. Permission was granted, and they told us that all along the river the guards had received orders the day before not to fight.

After Mr. Eden's arrival in the course of the day, intercourse was resumed in as friendly a manner as at the former camp, and oranges, fowls, eggs, pigs, Indian corn, &c., were brought in tolerable quantities. Preparations were immediately commenced by Captain Impey for bridging the Teesta.

On the 25th inst. I took a party to visit Neh, about two hours distant, a stronghold of great repute on our side (right bank) of the Teesta, which we found evacuated. Neh is at the end of a spur from Mount Mainom, and its strength consists in its being inaccessible from above, and terminating in a precipice near the river, besides a high scarped rock forming the greater part of the south side (the side of approach), leaving only a single path and a few places in that immediate neighbourhood by which it is at all accessible. All these ways of approach were well commanded from breastworks formed of large stones and heavy timbers. There were also at various points numbers of large rocks placed on the poise, with levers beside them, ready to roll down, and also a great many (as designated by the force) "booby traps," which we first became acquainted with at Sandoopchi, where they commanded the narrow and almost perpendicular path from Namchi.

These "traps" consist of three or more stout bamboos, about 5 feet long, placed about 6 or 8 feet apart, with one end resting against the side of the steep hill, and retained at a slight angle with the horizon by stout canes fastened to trees or rocks in rear. Across these are laid a few long bamboos, thus forming a sort of platform against which large stones and rocks are rested. Two or three men standing on the watch with their heavy knives cut the canes simultaneously, and the load is discharged down the hill. I can easily imagine that the moral effect produced by the noise of several tons of rocks crashing through the jungle would be very great, but, as Xenophon observed in a somewhat similar case, it is clear that the enemy would soon have no more rocks to roll.

To increase the difficulties of an attacking force, the enemy had cut and laid light and tangled underwood and bamboos at a short distance below the breastworks, across every line of approach, so that to struggle forward, to gain the shelter of some friendly tree or rock when a trap was discharged, would have been extremely difficult.

There is a "maidan" below well adapted for mortars, and I do not think that it would have been impossible, if executed

EMBARRASSING.

Current running fourteen "knots" below

with rapidity, to have turned the position by going along the bank of the river below the precipice, though this would expose a party so moving to a fire from the opposite bank, and the enemy on the top could be made aware of the movement, and the turning party might also be opposed by reinforcements of the enemy coming from Bhomsong Ghât. It might, however, supposing our force to be moving by the more northerly route *viâ* Neongong, be turned by a party in a two days' march round Mount Mainom. The north side presents nothing formidable.

We destroyed the stockades, discharged the traps, and returned to camp, where we found that 21 Sebundy Rifles, 10 sets of accoutrements, 2 Sebundy Sappers, Sepoys, and 1 Chuprassie had been given up; but I was informed by Mr. Eden that our preparations for bridging the Teesta were not approved of by the natives, and, on telling him of my intention to explore the road towards Tumloong the following day, he recommended my taking a stronger party than I had proposed.

I crossed the river the next day (26th) by the cane suspension bridge, and explored the road towards Tumloong *viâ* "Badong." The first ascent is very steep, but afterwards the road becomes very good, and, according to Cheboo Lama, continues so to Tumloong.

I was sorry to find all the villages deserted, and we passed several coolies laden with the baggage of Lamas and others proceeding towards Tumloong. On my return to camp I learned from Mr. Eden that most of the Kajees, with whom we had hitherto held communication, had left.

On the 27th inst. I again crossed the cane bridge to examine a lower road which keeps near the river up the left bank till near Bhomsong, when it ascends and meets the road which I had inspected on the previous day. The direction is very good, but it would take more time and labour than we can afford to render it equal to the upper road.

The villagers who had fled from our side (west) of the Teesta, were everywhere seen returning and crossing the river by rafts and bridges.* The speed and facility with which they construct a bridge is surprising. We here noticed a new style of bridge. It consisted,

1st. Of two parallel arches, say 10 or 12 feet apart, each constructed by securing a bundle of long bamboos (say 60 feet long) by the butts in the bank on either side of the river, and then bending them down across the river, making the thin ends overlap and tying them fast (an operation I was sorry that I did not witness).

2nd. From the two arches so formed are suspended bundles of bamboos firmly lashed together, and also arched slightly, forming the footway.

Two rails make all safe. It is far more comfortable than the suspension bridge, and it can be crossed easily by horses and cattle.

We crossed this bridge to the right bank and returned to camp.

Three or four Sepoys, the native doctor, a Bunnia, and a few articles of private property, were given up, and the Chota Dewan presented himself before the Special Commissioner.

Our bridge will be completed by Captain Impey either this evening or to-morrow.

A working party is improving the road up the hill. Coolies are expected to-morrow with fresh supplies.

I intend to leave at this point one company H.M. 6th Regiment and some native troops, and to place this post

* *i.e.* bridges north of our camp; I allowed no bridges between our camp and Took Ghât.

F. Stanford, Charing Cross

BAMBOO SUSPENSION BRIDGE AT THE TEESTA.

and Temi under the command of some intelligent officer, whom I shall direct to keep a strict watch, and to patrol constantly, and if necessary to destroy the rafts and bridges, which, at Mr. Eden's request, I have allowed to remain for the present, to enable the villagers to return to their homes.

The armed men have disappeared entirely, and there is every show of friendship, but I shall not forget that such people keep their word from self-convenience and not from principle, and that a check or disaster of any description, or sickness in the force, might make them view matters in a different light, and pay little regard to promises and professions into which they had been forced or frightened.

I propose leaving this for Tumloong with the force as below, with three weeks' provisions, so soon as the coolies with fresh supplies arrive. They are expected about the 1st or 2nd proximo.

	Officers.	N.C.O., Rank and File.
Royal Artillery	2 ..	30
H.M. 6th Regiment	5 ..	155
Baker's Sikhs	3 ..	112
Sebundy Sappers	1 ..	62
	2 Assistant Surgeons.	

I have, &c.,

J. C. GAWLER,

Lieut.-Colonel.

CHAPTER IV.

Instructions to Major Platt, in charge of post and bridge at Teesta—March 12th, Teesta bridge—road to Tumloong—review of operations—transport—resources of the country—climate—political—Thibet, produce, climate, &c.—Major Maitland—March 24th, expedition to the Chola Pass—table of elevations.

MEMORANDUM.

CAMP, RADOONG, TEESTA BRIDGE,
2ND MARCH, 1861.

MAJOR PLATT, H.M. 6th Foot, will have command of the line of operations from Temi to the Teesta bridge. He is reminded that, although matters are conducted with every show of friendship at present, the movers of the late hostilities against us made no overtures until they supposed their case hopeless.

Their friendship must therefore be looked upon as proceeding from present necessity, and their good faith can only be calculated upon so long as that necessity lasts; hence, a check or disaster, sickness in our force, want of provisions, or some great difficulty, might entirely alter their demeanour towards us, and cause them to foster whatever might harass or impede us, or even to commit direct acts of hostility, more or less open, according to the amount of danger or distress that we might be in.

Major Platt will keep himself informed of what is going on by patrolling the banks of the river, particularly near the bridge from above his present camp to the bridge below Temi at Took Ghât. Should any change of demeanour in the people be unmistakeable, all their bridges should be cut, and patrolling kept up incessantly. Convoys of provisions and return coolies should always be escorted, and parties from Temi and Namchi should meet each other half-way, and an officer should invariably accompany them; and thus, much information may be collected.

Should communication with the column be cut off, Major Platt will immediately report to Major Maitland, 79th Highlanders, commanding at Darjeeling, and is authorized, in case of emergency, to draw upon Namchi and the Rungeet for reinforcements.

His immediate business is the protection of the bridge, and the collecting and protection of supplies in transit from Namchi to the Teesta bridge.

Captain Cafe, Commissariat Officer at Namchi, has been directed to collect three weeks' supplies at the Teesta bridge as soon as coolies are available.

Major Platt will report regularly on Tuesdays and Saturdays, and anything special will be reported immediately.

Serjeant Dunn, Sebundy Sappers, with about twenty-five sappers and fifteen coolies from the Engineer Park will remain at the bridge; these will first be employed in throwing up a rough work at the bridge according to a plan which will be furnished by Captain Impey, Field Engineer, and will afterwards repair the road in the vicinity of the camp.

JOHN C. GAWLER,
Lieut.-Colonel, Commanding.

To the Qr. Mast. General of the Army.

CAMP, KABEE, NEAR TUMLOONG,
MARCH 12TH, 1861.

SIR,

In continuation of my letter of the 28th February, 1861, I have the honour to report, for the information of His Excellency the Commander-in-Chief, that the bridge across the Teesta was completed by Captain Impey, Field Engineer, on the same evening, with working parties of H.M. 6th Regiment, Baker's Sikhs, and the Sebundy Sappers. It was completed in twenty-eight actual working hours; its breadth is 8 feet and its length 212 feet, owing to its having to be carried over the immense rocks, which otherwise would almost prevent approach to the water's edge. It is a good, serviceable bridge, and will, Captain Impey thinks, stand anything short of a heavy flood.

On the morning of the 1st of March I moved the Royal Artillery, with two 12-pr. howitzers and 112 Baker's Sikhs, up the hill to a placed called "Pemiong," on a road which joins Rumtik and Tumloong, but keeping the western side of the mountain, at an average elevation of about 5000 feet above the Teesta. This route is not laid down by Dr. Campbell, but it passes through Yantong, from whence to Tumloong it is identical with the Bhomsong route.

	Bomr.	Grs.
Royal Artillery	1	4

	Officrs.	Serjt.	Rank and File.
H.M. 6th Regt.	1	—	50
Sikhs	1	—	9
Seby. Sappers	—	1	20

The arrival of supplies, as expected on the 2nd inst., more than completed me to three weeks, and I therefore moved up on the morning of the 3rd inst. with two companies H.M. 6th Regiment to Pemiong, leaving Major Platt, H.M. 6th Regiment, with force as per margin, in charge of the bridge. I gave him a memo. of instructions, a copy of which I annex.

On the 4th inst. I marched to Yantong; the greater part of the road was bad and rocky,—not so bad, though, but that horses and cattle passed it previous to its being improved, which was executed on the 4th and 5th insts. by the Sebundy Sappers and Engineer Park Coolies.

On the 6th and 7th insts. a company of the 6th moved forward a day's march to Munderra, a village situate on a spur on the left bank of the Ryott River, to enable the sappers to continue their work along the still bad and rocky road. The saddle and baggage horses of the officers passed without accident over this part also of the road previous to its being repaired.

The remainder of the force was halting meantime at Yantong, as I found it necessary to give the coolies a rest, and to draw up some supplies which had been left under a guard at Pemiong.

On the 8th inst. all joined at Munderra, and some "ticca" coolies having been obtained by Mr. Eden from the neighbouring villages, I was enabled to reach this camp with supplies, &c., complete, on the afternoon of the 9th inst. We are situated on the Choombi road, on a spur of the Chola Mountain, S.E. of Tumloong, in sight of and within an hour's walk of the Rajah's palace.

I have supplies to the 27th of this month, and there are large supplies at Namchi; I have sent back the coolies to bring them on to the Teesta, as I think it would be unwise to slacken preparations until matters have taken a *decided* turn.

The tobacco and boots will be here in a day or two.

REVIEW OF OPERATIONS.—My progress to this point has been slow, but I arrived here well supplied, and I have posts of communication well supplied and protected, good bridges, and good roads.*

It was the wish of His Excellency the Commander-in-Chief that the campaign should not be "a dash in and a dash out again," and my transport was insufficient for more. I have therefore moved forward step by step, never advancing to form another post until I had three weeks' supplies to maintain it; but by examining the country to considerable distances to the front and flanks, and making all movements with rapidity, I endeavoured to avoid the appearance of heaviness or shorthandedness, and, I think, succeeded so far as the enemy have been able to judge.

I was induced to commence operations with what His Excellency is aware I always considered inefficient transport, because I knew that with labour we should succeed; I saw little chance of its increasing or improving, and it was important not to delay, that in case of our having eventually to occupy the country, there should be time to arrange for the shelter and supply of the troops before the rains set in.

* Thanks to our excellent Field Engineer.

TRANSPORT. — I have never been favourable to coolie transport, and spoke in my last more approvingly of Dhanga coolies than I think now. From their mode of carrying loads slung on the shoulders of two men they require more turning room than a horse; and two of them carry about half one horse's load. In common with all coolies, each man requires the same weight of food to be carried for himself as one soldier requires; hence for a flying column they are almost useless. In addition to this, I find that the work in these hills for Dhangas is very severe, and they are unable to make three fair marches on three consecutive days if the route is hilly. Otherwise they are honest and easily controlled.*

To keep up a supply of provisions at posts I should employ Dhangas or "ticca" hill men; but a moveable column should have its mules or hill ponies, for each of which 1½ maund would be a light load. The pack-saddle should be of the Ordnance pattern in common use in Europe and the Cape. The pack-saddles or pads of India are almost useless in these hills, and are unfair upon the animals, frequently throwing them down by slipping with a jerk, although I have seen no paths here worse than *some* I have seen at the Cape; and my own pack-horse, with an Ordnance-pattern pack-saddle (the only one in the force), has never been down.†

RESOURCES OF THE COUNTRY.—The resources of the country are much greater than I had supposed; they have

* *Vide* p. 53.

† Towards the end of our march to our last standing camp at Kabee, the hill side, which was quite bare, was so steep that the path out of the Ryott River was zigzagged up to a considerable elevation. One of the mules carrying gun ammunition had nearly reached the top, when it slipped slightly on some wet ground which it was passing. The Indian *pack pad* allowed the ammunition boxes to *lurch*. Down came the mule on its side, one of the boxes burst, and shot and shell bounded playfully down the hill across the zigzags. It was amusing to witness the stimulating effect this discharge had on the movements of many below, who a moment before had seemed "half done."

brought in onions and spinach;* they have also buckwheat, rice, and Indian corn, pigs, goats, fowls, and eggs. There are also some herds of cattle, which have been concealed in the jungle, where I have seen them.

It is but natural that the inhabitants should at present conceal their supplies, as they probably cannot understand a force maintaining itself. I annex a list of prices paid in camp for articles of food obtained from the natives.†

CLIMATE.—We have experienced no cold except near the summit of Mount Tendong, where the snow lay in small patches in the jungle, and a cold mist hung over us night and day. In the valleys of the Rungeet and Teesta it is always warm, and frequently uncomfortably close; but at Namchi, Temi, and camps at about 5000 feet elevation, it is extremely pleasant. It is getting warmer, however, and the valley of the Teesta will in about three weeks become unhealthy. I shall then move the European guard to a higher elevation, above the bridge, and keep a detachment of natives at the bridge head. We had rain for the first time on the 9th inst. at this camp, but no more is expected for five or six weeks, at the setting in of the rains.

POLITICAL.—The Rajah's son arrived yesterday from Choombi. His journey occupied five days, and the snow was said to be very deep in the Chola Pass. His escort consisted of about forty men armed with guns, and twenty or thirty coolies carrying supplies. They took a circuitous route to avoid passing through the camp. He rode on a man's back the greater part of the way, and was dressed in bright yellow; on reaching the face of the hill

* Thus in the original. I cannot recollect whether this is a little fun, or whether our diet of beef, rice, and biscuit caused us to give these vegetables a greedy welcome.

† I have not a copy of this.

opposite the camp, he changed his dress to blue and mounted a mule.

By some he is called the Rajah; but the case is peculiar, and not unlike a subterfuge frequently resorted to by savages and semi-civilized nations to prevent responsibility being fixed on anyone.

About seven years ago, the Dewan being out of office, and in disgrace (I believe for Dr. Campbell's and Dr. Hooker's affair), the old Rajah abdicated and appointed his son (the one now here) Rajah, and made another man his Dewan (the present Chota Dewan); shortly afterwards the old Dewan reappeared, and without much ceremony resumed his office, and the old Rajah and he transacted business as usual. The recent affair with Dr. Campbell was transacted by the Dewan and the old Rajah, and the Chiefs and Kajees acknowledged the right, for they obeyed the summons.

Under these circumstances, the old Rajah cannot well punish, banish, or surrender the Dewan; moreover, he is married to the Dewan's sister.*

There are still one Havildar, fourteen Sepoys, and several Chuprassies and servants unaccounted for, also forty rifles, some Government tents, and sundry other property, public and private, not given up. Mr. Eden anticipates that everything will be settled in ten days, when it is proposed that we return by the Linsing Ghât road (described in Dr. Campbell's route) to the Teesta, and thence *viâ* Yongong (or Neongong), Pemionchi, Rinchingpoong, and Goke to Darjeeling. Should compliance with our demands be delayed, the approaching rains may make our position difficult.

THIBET.—We are now two marches from the Chola Pass, the Thibet frontier; thence it is three marches to Choombi,

* So far from being punished or banished, he is now (1873) Governor of Choombi. There is no doubt that he is an energetic man, and it is to be hoped that he is a wiser one than he was between 1849 and 1861.

which, though in Thibet, has long been the Sikhim Head Quarters.

SEASON.—I am informed that the pass is practicable almost all the year round; that just now it is bad (and yet the Rajah's son has crossed it), but in four or five weeks when the Sikhim rains begin, it will be quite clear from snow and will remain so for five or six months. The country on the other side of the Pass is not subject to the heavy summer or hot-weather rains.

ASPECT.—The country is described as undulating, like that at the foot of our hills, covered with long grass, and almost devoid of timber. Great people buy firewood, others burn sheep and cattle dung.

PRODUCE.*—Horses, mules, cattle, and sheep are in abundance; of the latter there are as many as 7000 or 8000 in the flock of a single village. Grain and other supplies are described as one-third the price in Choombi that they are at Darjeeling. Choombi is described as a large city with bazaars.

ROADS.—Roads are described as being very good, "fit for carts," and along the road from Choombi to Lhassa it is said a carriage could be driven.

CONCLUSION.—For the safe and prosperous condition in which I now find myself with regard to supplies and important arrangements in rear, I am much indebted to Major Maitland, 79th Highlanders, in whose charge I left them, with command and general supervision as far as Namchi, giving him, as well as I could foresee, an outline of my intentions. He has been unremitting in his exertions to carry

* For articles of commerce, *vide* p. 105.

out my wishes, and has enabled me to move forward with a confidence which I could not otherwise have possessed.

I have received every assistance from the Staff and Regimental Officers of the Force, but would specially recommend to the notice of His Excellency the Commander-in-Chief, Lieut. Fryer, 2nd R.B., Officiating Brigade-Major. This officer has shown great ability, and by his assiduous attention has afforded me great assistance. Also Lieut. Delafosse, with whose previous career His Excellency must be already acquainted, and who has proved himself an energetic, enterprising, and intelligent officer.

I have, &c.,

JOHN C. GAWLER,

Lieut.-Colonel, Commanding Sikhim Field Force.

Note.—While preliminaries to the Treaty and other matters were being discussed and arranged by the Envoy and ministers of the Rajah, I left our camp near Tumloong, at about nine o'clock one night, and proceeded with Captain Murray to inspect our line of communication, roads, bridges, posts, and supplies. Picking up fresh ponies at the Teesta and at Namchi, we reached Darjeeling at six o'clock the next evening. A glance at the map and the table of elevations will show that this was pretty fair going, and indicates the vast improvements that had been effected by the road parties under Captain Impey's directions. We returned to Tumloong in the next forty-eight hours.

The Qr. Mast. General of the Army.

SIR, CAMP KABEE, MARCH 24TH, 1861.

I have the honour to report, for the information of His Excellency the Commander-in-Chief, that on the 16th inst. I was informed by Mr. Eden that a period of five days, which had been allowed to the Rajah within which to comply with our demands, had expired, and that a second similar period had that morning been granted.

Taking advantage of the time thus afforded, I therefore, with Mr. Eden's acquiescence, made arrangements for visiting the Chola Pass. He informed me that it was part of the treaty that we should be "free of the country," and that though the Thibet frontier guard had been doubled, they had sent to him to say that he must think nothing of it, as it was a mere matter of military precaution.

On the afternoon of the 17th inst. I started with a party of officers; our baggage having been sent forward by coolies and pack-horse, with a small escort. We halted for the night at Pomunting, a sort of grassy knoll, about two hours' walk from Kabee. There is a small spring of water here, but it was barely sufficient at this season for our party (horses not included), but in the rains it would be pretty plentiful.

The road is very accurately described in Hooker's work, vol. ii., pages 196–200. It keeps the ridge on which Kabee is situated for a considerable distance. It is now rough and rocky, but might with little labour be made very good. To Phieungong it is generally very steep. Between Pomunting and Laghep, water might be obtained by digging in one or two places, and from Laghep upwards snow lies in the jungles more or less until the rains. There is plenty of bamboo for horses and cattle, and some patches of good grass.

From Phieungong the road keeps the top of the ridge,

which undulates slightly for about a mile and a half (bamboos cease, and the grass is frost-bitten at this season), and then inclines down to the right into a small valley, where there are plenty of fir trees, and a good stream of water running south into the Rutto River. Here we encamped for the night of the 18th. The journey from Pomunting took me four, and the coolies five and a half, hours.

From our camp of the 18th the road leads through fir forests, with occasionally open grassy patches, up the Rutto River through Barfonchen to Chumanako, where we halted on the 19th. The march occupied two and a half hours, and for coolies three and a half. The northern slopes in this valley were covered with snow, the southern quite free, with the exception occasionally of patches behind rocks and trees. Chumanako is at the mouth of a wide rocky gorge, up which the path could be traced for some distance.

The Chola Pass was said by our guide to be three hours distant, but it was not my intention to visit it, as on the evening of the 17th I had received a note from Mr. Eden, wherein he stated: "The people here are very apprehensive "of your party coming to words with the Thibet frontier "guards . . . . . . It would be imprudent to go beyond "Chumanako, or let the Thibet guards even hear of your "presence, as they suspect that we have come here with "ultimate designs on them, and might think you had come "to reconnoitre."

On the afternoon of the 19th I strolled out in the direction of the Pass, and was surprised to find the path very good, and notwithstanding that the snow in the Pass was reported to be nearly 3 feet deep, several parties of heavily laden coolies passed our camp, both towards and from the Pass. About twenty minutes beyond Chumanako, fir trees and all vegetation disappear.

I was on the point of returning, after walking leisurely for an hour and a half, and visiting some frozen lakes, when we came suddenly in sight of some poles with flags on them, at a distance of about 200 yards. A sentry, in red, was sitting against a rock, with his back towards us, at the top of a wide gorge on the eastern side of the range. We retired without being seen, and an hour's walk brought us back to camp.

The next morning, as the remainder of the party were desirous of visiting the Pass, and as from the continual passing and repassing of coolies, the Thibet guard must have been from the first well aware of our movements, I sent the baggage back towards Kabee, and started at seven o'clock for the Pass, which we reached at half-past eight o'clock. Captain Murray brought his horse to the top, and rode nearly the whole way. The guard was this time on the alert, and told our guide that they would be very happy to see us at the boundary, but they had orders not to come a foot on our side, and to allow no European to go a foot on theirs. They sent us, by our guide, some fire, and showed him the seal of the Emperor of China.

I held no further conversation with them, and only waited about twenty minutes. We descended again, breakfasted at twelve o'clock at our halting place of the 18th, and then proceeding on with some of the party, I reached Kabee at 3½ P.M. the same day; and our pack-horses arrived about two hours afterwards without accident.

In no place on the path in the Pass was the snow more than ankle deep, and even at the top the south faces of the mountains were free from snow (*vide* Hooker, vol. ii., p. 199). There was no extreme cold. Some of the party thought they experienced shortness of breath, and one complained of headache.

I have, &c.,

JOHN C. GAWLER,

Lieut.-Colonel, Commanding Sikhim Field Force.

To convey an idea of the country from Punkabarri to Tumloong and Chola Pass, the following Table has been framed from the elevations given by Dr. Hooker, 'Himalayan Journals,' Appendix, vol. ii.:—

	feet.
Punkabarri	1815
Kursiong	4813
Sinchul (barracks of the 6th Regiment)	8655
Darjeeling	7100
Guard-house above Rungeet	1864
Bed of Rungeet at cane bridge (our crossing point)	818
Mikh	3912
Namchi	5608
Tendong	8671
Temi	4771
Bhomsong (Ghât on Teesta, about 4 miles above our bridge)	1556
Tumloong	5368
Laghep	10423
Phieungong	12422
Barfonchen	11233
Chumanako	12590
Chola Pass	14925

OTHER ELEVATIONS ON RETURN ROUTE.

Neongong Monastery	5225
Pass from Teesta to Rungeet	6824
Lingdam village	5349
Rungeet River (on route to Rinchingpoong)	1805
Little Rungeet Guard, near Goke	1672

CHAPTER V.

April 9th, Durbar and signature of Treaty — break up camp — Linsing Ghât road — reach the Teesta—cross the range to Rinchingpoong — position in which Governor-General's Agent was attacked — native method of advance against the stockade — Dr. Campbell's services — April 27, breaking up the force — troops — ordnance — tents — Lieut. Becher—Conclusion.

To the Qr. Mast. General of the Army.

SIR, DARJEELING, APRIL 9TH, 1861.

I have the honour to report, for the information of His Excellency the Commander-in-Chief, that the Durbar and signature of the Treaty took place at Tumloong, on the 29th ultimo.*

* Some particulars of this ceremony from Mr. Eden's final report may be interesting. For Treaty, *vide* p. 100.

Para. 26. "On the 29th February, the Treaty was signed in a monastery "near the Rajah's house, in the presence of all the officers of the force. The "Treaty was read out by Colonel Gawler in English to the European troops; "in Hindu by my moonshee to the native troops; and by the Chotah Dewan "in Bootiah to the natives of the country, a large assemblage of whom crowded "round to listen to it. The troops were then marched past; a royal salute "was fired, and a salute was also fired for the Rajah.

27. "The Rajah and his Umlah were evidently much struck by the appear- "ance of the troops, more especially of the Europeans: most of those present "had never seen a European force before.

29. "After the Treaty was signed, presents were interchanged."

These presents were a mere matter of form. They were sold on behalf of the Government, and our return presents were made at Government expense. If I recollect right, the Rajah's present to me consisted of a large pile of woollen cloth of Thibet manufacture, one or two yaks, and a white-faced pony. My return present consisted of one of our 100-lb. tins of biscuit, which would certainly try their teeth, and a barrel of rum, to show him how we lived in the field. Both were opened and tried all round by several Lamas and Kajees; the rum gave much satisfaction. It tasted to them perhaps as a liqueur; their own arrack is considerably above proof and has a very disagreeable flavour, and is I fancy expensive. After being tasted, the tin and keg were closed up, sealed, and sent off immediately to the Maharajah at Choombi.

By moving forward troops from the Teesta and supplying their place from posts in rear, I was enabled, after leaving in camp at Kabee sufficient guards from each detatchment, to have present at the Durbar force as per margin.

	Rank and File.
Royal Artillery	20
Two 12-pr. howitzers.	
H.M. 6th Royals ..	160
Baker's Sikhs	80
Sebundy Sappers ..	40

On the following day I broke up camp, and, with Mr. Eden's acquiescence, proceeded with 50 rank and file H.M. 6th Regiment and 50 Sikhs towards the Teesta, by the Linsing Ghât road, sending Major Platt, commanding H.M. 6th, back by our old road with the remainder of the force, and supplies, of which we had a fortnight's in hand. The rain fell in torrents during the nights of the 31st ult. and 1st inst.

The country through which we passed had more cultivation than we had hitherto seen.

The road was bad, and I consider it a bad line of communication with Tumloong. It crosses numerous spurs with very steep ascents and descents; it is intricate, and the valleys at this season, and even earlier, are hot and unhealthy. Both its flanks are exposed, and it would require either numerous posts, or large escorts for the protection of convoys.

The road by which we had marched to Tumloong, after ascending direct from the Teesta to an elevation of about 5000 feet, keeps pretty much the same level, and has its left flank covered by the Teesta and Ryott rivers, until towards the end of the last march, when it descends to cross the Ryott. Moreover, from a point near Yantong, at the angle above the junction of the Teesta and Ryott, nearly the whole line of road, to the Teesta bridge on the one side and to Kabee and Tumloong on the other side, is under the eye. Had matters looked less favourable, I should have had a block-house built at this point.

I arrived at the Teesta on the 2nd inst., and found that Major Platt and a great part of the stores had crossed. Mr. Eden had proceeded to Darjeeling, and had intimated to me by letter that it would have a good effect if some of the troops were to march round by Rinchingpoong. I therefore halted at the Teesta during the 3rd inst. to make arrangements and to leave final instructions with Major Platt.

On the 4th inst. I proceeded with 50 rank and file H.M. 6th Royals and 50 rank and file Baker's Sikhs past the Neongong Monastery to the head of the Rungpo River, at the foot of the pass on the Teesta side of the range which separates the Teesta and the Rungeet rivers.

On the 5th I crossed the range and pushed on across the Rungeet, as the heavy rains that had fallen nearly every night since we left Tumloong rendered every delay a risk.

On the 6th inst. I put the camp in motion, and, as the road was now clear, and the remaining rivers securely bridged, I handed over command to Captain Kendall, H.M. 6th Regiment, with the necessary instructions, and, accompanied by Captain Murray, proceeded through Rinchingpoong, Zung, and Goke, to Darjeeling, where I arrived at 9.30 P.M.

The road commenced by my orders to Goke now nearly joins that which was cut by Dr. Campbell to Rinchingpoong.

At Rinchingpoong I stayed about two hours, and examined the position in which Dr. Campbell had been attacked. It was an open hillock, commanded within easy musket shot on two sides by high ground covered with jungle, and, on the other sides, approach could be made to within half-musket shot under cover of a steep bank also covered with jungle. The water was out of sight of, though at no great distance from, Dr. Campbell's stockade, but was commanded by the high ground before mentioned, and was consequently in the possession of the attacking force.

I saw fifty or sixty boards in the neighbourhood of the

stockade, which had been used by the enemy as shields behind which they advanced to the attack. The boards were about 5 ft. 8 in. × 2 ft. 3 in., and were from 2½ to 3 inches in thickness. Sticks secured with cane formed the handles. Several had bullet holes in them, and in one I counted four, of which only two had passed through.

There were several places where human bodies had been burned, it being the custom of this people to burn the bones of their dead.

Within 800 yards of Dr. Campbell's stockade was a very good position, which secured the water and all ground around it. On two sides there was open ground for long musket shot, a third side was precipitous, and on a fourth it was approachable only by a narrow ridge. I understand, however, that they would have been unable to move their stores to that distance in time; and, in any case, their ammunition not being sufficient to last out another night, the posting of strong pickets of the enemy on their line of communication with Darjeeling, and the information that that place was attacked, would have decided their retreat.

The road from the Rungeet to the Teesta, commenced by my orders when I entered Sikhim, has been finished; and I should recommend that every effort should now be made to finish the new cart-road between Darjeeling and Punkabarri, which will render the Government and the public less at the mercy of the coolies than they now are.

The whole of the European troops who have been employed on the expedition are within British territory to-day; and in two or three days more the remainder of the stores and rear guard will have been withdrawn from Sikhim.

As the expedition is now at an end, and I have received His Excellency's instructions for the breaking-up of the force, I feel it my duty to express my best thanks to Dr.

Campbell, Superintendent of Darjeeling, on whom rested the responsibility of the transport. In January, previous to the departure of the expedition, when doubts were entertained as to whether the coolies were to be depended on, Dr. Campbell expressed to Mr. Eden, Assistant Commissary-General Fitz-Gerald, and myself his readiness to accompany the coolies into Sikhim sooner than that any failure should be risked.

The management of the hill coolies, I have learned by experience, is of a difficult and delicate nature. They are, I have before remarked, at once timid and independent; the Coolie Corps was unpopular, and the coolies disliked the idea of accompanying the column, consequently its numbers never materially increased and frequent desertions took place.

On the Teesta, at the end of February, Lieut. Becher, commanding the Coolie Corps, had considerable difficulty in inducing the coolies to cross; and, although a month's pay was due, sixteen deserted.

Dr. Campbell's exertions, notwithstanding, procured coolies and bullocks to keep up the supplies in rear. When the force reached the Teesta, he procured "ticca" coolies to go to Namchi, and when I advanced to Tumloong he induced them to go to the Teesta, thus keeping supplies always within my reach, so that when I broke up my camp at Kabee on the 30th March, I had a fortnight's supplies in hand; there were upwards of three weeks' supplies at the Teesta, and five weeks' more at Namchi.

Besides this, Dr. Campbell had the entire feeding of the Coolie Corps, including the original hill men, and latterly 250 Dhanga coolies. The supplies for the latter had to be procured from the plains and forwarded to the column, and had these failed for a single day the consequences would have been serious.

I have frequently brought to His Excellency's notice the services rendered me by Major Maitland, commanding Convalescent Depôt, whose judicious arrangements in my rear relieved me of much anxiety.

I beg also to express my thanks to Major Platt, H.M. 6th Regiment, for the activity he displayed when in command of the Teesta bridge, in carrying out my instructions, and also, employed as he now is, in superintending the withdrawal of the remaining troops and stores from Sikhim.

To Lieutenant Roberts, commanding Royal Ártillery of the Force, who is an active and intelligent officer, and thoroughly acquainted with his profession.

To Captain Baker, commanding Military Police, who was ever ready, and to whose qualifications for command the smartness at all times and good behaviour of his men testified.

To Captain Impey, Field Engineer to the Force, whose services on various occasions I have brought to the notice of His Excellency.

To Captain Murray, commanding Sebundy Sappers, Assistant Superintendent, whose numerous vocations, civil and military, rendered his position extremely difficult, but who, nevertheless, carried out with energy and spirit all I required of him.

The assistance which I have always received from my personal Staff has already elicited His Excellency's approval.

I have, &c.,

J. C. GAWLER,

Lieut.-Col., commanding Sikhim Field Force.

The Qr. Mast. General of the Army.

SIR, DARJEELING, APRIL 27TH, 1861.

I have the honour to report for the information of STORES. His Excellency the Commander-in-Chief, that the whole of the stores belonging to the Sikhim Field Force were removed within our frontier on the 15th instant, and were stored at Darjeeling on the 23rd instant.

TROOPS. — The wing 3rd Sikh Infantry left this on the 15th instant, en route to the Punjaub. I was obliged to detain Captain Renny, commanding this corps, as being President of the Court of Inquiry, whose proceedings were not terminated, and member of a District Court Martial, not dissolved.

The detachment Royal Artillery have left Sinchul this day. On account of the prevalence of cholera* in the neighbourhood of Punkabarri I thought it advisable to detain them until the elephants sent up for them were reported at the foot of the hills. These elephants have brought up two detachments of invalids; the 1st arrived at the depôt on the 24th, and the 2nd, with forty men unable to march, out of a detachment of fifty, reached Punkabarri yesterday. Hence the road is much crowded, and our limited transport much taxed.

Ten men of the detachment Royal Artillery remain at Darjeeling, at the recommendation of a medical committee.

The detachment of H.M. 19th Regiment, under Major Jennings, from Titalyah, will arrive at Sinchul this day (27th).

The wing 73rd N.I., except fifty rank and file retained to escort ordnance and other stores down country, will march in a day or two. Their carriage is ready at the foot of the hills, but they require coolie carriage from this.

ORDNANCE.—I propose retaining the Mountain Train Battery and two mortars, sent from the Allahabad Arsenal, and returning to Calcutta Arsenal all the remaining guns which I had originally proposed keeping (letter 177, 16th inst., to Adjutant-General of the Army), but which I find to be

* *Vide* Postscript.

mostly of dissimilar descriptions or requiring repairs, *viz.*: two 12-pr. howitzers, lately used in Sikhim, carriages much shaken and requiring repairs. Two 12-pr. howitzers, Naval Brigade, difference of calibre, no sights, double-cheeked trails. One 12-pr. howitzer, belonging to Sebundy Sappers, heavy, and not adapted for mountain work, double-cheeked trail. Two 2-pr. guns belonging to Sebundy Sappers, carriage of one double cheeked. One 3-pr. gun at Convalescent Depôt. One 3-pr. gun, injured, no carriage, lately given up by the Sikhim Government. I have further ordered 200 rounds per gun to be retained for the Mountain Train Battery and mortars, and all remaining to be returned into the Calcutta magazine, also rockets which I found unserviceable.* I have given directions regarding small-arm ammunition, agreeably to instructions contained in your letter of the 4th April, 1861.

Committees have sat on all guns, ammunition, and other stores, ordnance and medical, furnished to the Sikhim Field Force; invoices have been prepared and receipts given for:—

> Guns, rockets, and ammunition, by Lieut. Beavan, d.d., Sebundy Sappers;
> Entrenching tools, by Captain Murray, commanding Sebundy Sappers;
> Medical stores, by Dr. Drysdale, Convalescent Depôt.

TENTS.—Concerning tents I have given orders, agreeably to instructions contained in paragraph 7 of your letter of the 4th inst.; but recommend that they be kept in store at Titalyah instead of at Punkabarri, and that an active warrant officer, or some proper person, be sent to take charge of the store at Titalyah, which has hitherto (for about six years) been kept by the Department Public Works, and it has been the practice with invalids, or other troops marching up and down the road, to draw tents from or return them into store at Titalyah, by requisition on the Department

* These rockets had been a long time in store and had deteriorated. They used to describe very disagreeable curves instead of going straight. I had specially asked for them, as I had seen excellent practice with rockets during the Kaffir War.

Public Works. Much inconvenience, and probable loss or damage to Government property has resulted from this irregular custom; and lengthy correspondence with the Executive Engineer will hereafter be forwarded.

APPOINTMENTS.—The following appointments have appeared in Orders as having ceased:—

Field Engineer.
Two Assistant Field Engineers.
Field Surgeon.
Three Assistants to Coolie Corps.

The Coolie Corps will be disbanded on the 30th inst., when the appointment of Lieut. Becher will cease.

I beg to take this opportunity of expressing my best thanks to Lieut. Becher, who has managed the coolies with great firmness, patience, tact, and perseverance. I trust His Excellency will appreciate this officer's services, as less zeal on his part might have placed us in serious difficulties.

Arrangements as above having been made, and it being now a mere matter of time to send the remaining troops and stores down the road, and to collect the necessary carriage from the neighbouring districts, I propose handing over the command on Tuesday, the 30th inst., when the appointment of Lieut. Fryer, R.B., as Brigade-Major, will cease.

I have, &c.,

JOHN C. GAWLER,
Lieut.-Colonel, Commanding at Darjeeling.

APRIL 28TH.

P.S.—Letter from Quartermaster-General's Office, No. 1494, received last night, and instructions despatched immediately to the Officer Commanding Detachment Royal Artillery.

CONCLUSION.

Some, who may have taken the trouble to glance over these papers, may think that, from the amount of opposition therein shown to have been encountered, there is an exhibition of exertion, and perhaps of precaution, in excess of what the enemy deserved.

It would, however, have been a serious responsibility if the life of a single man had been lost through the omission of any exertion or precaution that might reasonably have been used; and the amount of "fight" shown by any enemy, particularly by the less civilized, depends less upon any formidable qualities he may possess, than upon the opportunities you may offer him of exercising those powers with effect. The French army in 1796, by a few manœuvres, forced the Piedmontese *without fighting* to abandon positions, in *attacking* which in 1793 it had lost the *élite* of its grenadiers *without attaining* its object.

The fighting portion of the enemy in the present case were Bhooteas and Thibeteans. Of the qualifications of the former, it is sufficient to say that we have had a Bhootan war and a medal. As regards the latter, they are grave, stern-looking men, and their physique is splendid, — far superior to the Chinese,—and there is no reason for supposing that they were not in courage, discipline, and equipment fully equal to the Chinese, whom we have encountered at various times in a much less difficult country.

APPENDIX.

General Orders — Extract from Instructions of Government — Extract from final Report of the Hon. Ashley Eden — Report of Captain Impey, Field Engineer — Extract from Treaty — Memo. by Colonel Gawler and Dr. Campbell, May, 1873 — Trade of Thibet.

There were several officers whose names were accidentally omitted from the following General Orders, but were subsequently published. Among them were Major Fitz-Gerald, A.C.G., and Surgeon-Major Keats, M.D.

(No. 73 of 1861. Military Department.)

To the Right Honourable Sir Charles Wood, Bart., Her Majesty's Secretary of State for India.

Sir,

We have the honour to transmit, for the information of Her Majesty's Government, the accompanying copy of correspondence regarding the recent operations in Sikhim, which have been brought to a close successfully, and with much credit to the officer who commanded the expedition.

We have expressed in a General Order, copy of which forms one of the enclosures of this letter, our sense of the ability, energy, and good judgment with which the operations were conducted by Lieut.-Colonel Gawler, of the assistance rendered to him by the officers whom he has specially mentioned, and of the services and good conduct of the whole of the expeditionary force.

We have, &c.,

(Signed) CANNING.
H. ROSE.
J. B. W. FRERE.
R. NAPIER.

FORT WILLIAM, 8TH MAY, 1861.

FROM THE ADJUTANT-GENERAL OF THE ARMY TO THE SECRETARY TO THE GOVERNMENT OF INDIA MILITARY DEPARTMENT, 15TH APRIL, 1861.

SIR,

In forwarding for submission to Government the final Report of the operations of the Sikhim Field Force, I am instructed by the Commander-in-Chief to take the opportunity of drawing the especial attention of His Excellency the Governor-General in Council to the admirable tact and judgment with which the operations in question have been uniformly conducted by Lieut.-Colonel J. C. Gawler, H.M. 73rd Regiment, who commanded the expedition.

2. Although the force under Colonel Gawler met with little opposition, too much praise cannot, in Sir Hugh Rose's opinion, be accorded to him for having so skilfully

carried out his instructions and brought the undertaking to a successful issue.

3. I am further to request you will solicit the attention of Government to the services of the officers of the expedition who were more particularly useful to Lieut.-Colonel Gawler.

I have, &c.,

W. MAYHEW,

Lieut.-Colonel, Adjutant-General of the Army.

(No. 552.)

GENERAL ORDER BY H.E. THE GOVERNOR-GENERAL OF INDIA IN COUNCIL, NO. 440, DATED FORT WILLIAM, 14TH MAY, 1861.

The operations in Sikhim having been brought to a close, and the expeditionary force having returned to British territory and been broken up, the Right Honourable the Governor-General in Council desires to record his approbation of the good services of the force, and of their soldier-like conduct in the field.

The ability, energy, and good judgment displayed by Lieut.-Colonel Gawler in bringing these military operations to a successful issue, carried on as they were in a difficult and mountainous country, are highly appreciated by the Governor-General in Council.

The services rendered to Lieut.-Colonel Gawler's force by Dr. Campbell, Superintendent of Darjeeling, and the services of Major Maitland, commanding the Convalescent Depôt, of Major Platt, Her Majesty's 6th Regiment, of Captain Impey and Lieut. Carter, of the Bengal Engineers, Captain Murray, commanding Sebundy Sappers, Captain Baker, commanding Bengal Military Police, and of Lieutenants Roberts, Royal Artillery, Delafosse, late 53rd Native Infantry, Fryer, Brigade-Major, and Beavan, Sebundy Sappers, and Serjeant Dunne, also of the Sebundy Sappers, and Serjeants Dickson and O'Hara, of the Sappers and Miners, have been brought to the notice of Government by Lieut.-Colonel Gawler.

The energy and valuable services rendered by Lieut. Pierson, of the Bengal Engineers, and by Sub-Lieutenant Hidyat Alli, of the Bengal Military Police, have been specially brought to the notice of Government.

To these officers and men, to all the officers, European and native, and to the non-commissioned officers and soldiers of the force, His Excellency in Council offers his best thanks for the manner in which their duties on this occasion have been discharged.

INSTRUCTIONS. (Extract.)

FROM THE OFFICIATING SECRETARY TO THE GOVERNMENT OF INDIA TO THE HON. ASHLEY EDEN.

SIR, CAMP, REWAH, 28TH DEC., 1860.

I am directed by the Governor-General to inform you that His Excellency has been pleased to select you to fill the part of Envoy and Special Commissioner in Sikhim.

2. The object of your appointment, which is a temporary one, is to exact from the Rajah of Sikhim, or from the actual governing authority of that State, satisfaction for insults and injuries done to British subjects, and for violation of British territory.

3. Some months ago demands to this effect were made upon the Rajah. These demands were not satisfied, and the Superintendent of Darjeeling was authorized to occupy a part of the Rajah's territory as a means of compelling satisfaction.

4. The occupation was proceeded with, but not successfully. The force with which it was attempted was insufficient; and from this and other causes that force was unable to hold its position, and the Superintendent and the force together were compelled to retire within British territory, with some loss of men and stores. The retreat of the force has been followed by insolent threatenings, and, in some instances, by transgressions of our frontier on the part of hostile bands of Sikhimites. By the last accounts these demonstrations still continued in the neighbourhood of Darjeeling.

5. You will find the force which is now being concentrated at Darjeeling, in the command of Lieut.-Colonel

Gawler, of H.M. 73rd Regiment, an officer of tried experience in dealing with an uncivilized enemy.

8. The atonement which has already been demanded from the Rajah for the plundering, maltreating, and kidnapping of British subjects, and for the violation of British territory, is to be exacted.

9. The discredit which we have suffered by the ineffectual attempt at coercion, and by the retreat of the Superintendent and of the force which accompanied him, must be removed, and an end must be put to the presumption which manifestly it has engendered in the Rajah's people.

EXTRACT FROM FINAL REPORT OF THE HON. A. EDEN, ENVOY AND SPECIAL COMMISSIONER IN SIKHIM, NO. 40, APRIL 8TH, 1861, TO THE SECRETARY TO GOVERNMENT OF BENGAL.

Para. 39. Colonel Gawler will doubtless have brought to notice the excellent conduct of the troops through the usual channel. Before concluding this Report, however, I cannot resist the inclination to add my testimony to this effect.

40. It is true that there has been but little fighting, but this, I think, will not be considered by His Excellency the Viceroy as in any way detracting from the claims of the troops to his favourable consideration. The days have happily passed away when the manner in which a force has performed its duty is estimated solely by the length of the list of killed and wounded.

41. To a soldier there is no greater pleasure than fighting, and to say that he has fought bravely is so much a matter of course with the British soldier, that it can scarcely be considered a compliment.

42. If anything, the absence of fighting in a country like Sikhim is an additional claim of the soldier to consideration, for it is a grievous disappointment superadded to his other hardships. The hope of an engagement with an enemy will sustain many men through difficulties which they would shrink from without this stimulus. It appears to me, then, that if it can be shown that the men composing a force have gone through great hardships and privations; that they have marched through what they believed to be an enemy's country without doing violence to either persons or property; that they have uniformly conducted themselves in a foreign land in such a manner as to reflect credit on their country and gain the goodwill of the country, they have deserved the approbation of the Government they serve even in a greater degree than if they had fought a hard fight. In the former case, they would be acting under a generous self-restraint; in the latter, they would merely obey a natural instinct. That the Europeans and natives of the Sikhim Field Force have thus conducted themselves, I can with great pleasure affirm. From the date on which they distinctly understood our position as regards the inhabitants, they passed through villages filled with men, women, and children, without doing the slightest injury to a single individual. One act of violence would have driven all the inhabitants into the jungles; one instance of hastiness or ill-treatment would have deprived us of all our transport; but the conduct of the troops was such that men who had been taught to consider them in the light of savages, soon learnt to mix with them and remain without apprehension in the camp. From the date on which the troops left Sinchul to the date of their return, not a man has been under any cover, night or day, except such as was afforded by boughs of trees. The men had neither tents nor great-coats. They marched, in several instances, night and day, through a country which Brigadier

Young, in 1850, pronounced impracticable for troops. Whatever hardships the men went through were fully shared by Colonel Gawler and the officers. During the two months we were in Sikhim I never saw a single case of drunkenness amongst the men. Captain Baker's Sikhs, in addition to their other privations, had no atta during the greater portion of their stay in Sikhim; they however bore this exceedingly well. They did their full share of the work, and rendered valuable assistance in the construction of bridges. Sub-Lieutenant Hidyat Alli, of that corps, not only rendered great assistance in this way, but was very useful to me in obtaining information and in communicating with the natives.

THE QR. MAST. GENERAL OF THE ARMY.

SIR, DARJEELING, APRIL 24TH, 1861.

I have the honour herewith to forward, for the information of His Excellency the Commander-in-Chief, the Report of Captain Impey, Field Engineer to the Sikhim Field Force, on the various works executed by his department during the expedition, many of which have already been brought by myself to His Excellency's notice.

I fully concur in the opinion Captain Impey has expressed concerning Lieutenants Pierson and Carter, B.E., and the works and surveys executed by them, as also in the mention he has made of Sub-Lieutenant Hidyat Alli, 1st Battalion Military Police. This officer has frequently attracted my notice by his intelligence, zeal, and personal exertions, whether on the march or with working parties, affording the best example to those under him, and the greatest support to his commanding officer.

The map alluded to by Captain Impey I shall shortly have the honour of presenting to His Excellency in Calcutta.

I have, &c.,

JOHN C. GAWLER, Lieut.-Colonel,
H.M. 73rd Regt., commanding Sikhim Field Force.

FROM CAPTAIN ARCHIBALD IMPEY, CHIEF ENGINEER SIKHIM FIELD FORCE, TO LIEUT.-COLONEL GAWLER, BRIGADIER COMMANDING SIKHIM FIELD FORCE.

SIR, DARJEELING, APRIL 10TH, 1861.

The field force under your command having returned from Sikhim, the object for which it was assembled having been accomplished, I have now the honour of reporting to you the several duties that were performed by my contingent of your force.

2. The operations devolving on the Engineer Department involved the bridging of three considerable hill streams, the Great Rungeet, the Teesta, and the Rumaam, the opening out of roads for the force, and in one instance the erection of buildings for the storage and protection of stores.

3. On my arrival at Darjeeling I found that no sapper serjeants, to assist me in taking charge of the Engineer Park, had arrived; in fact that the Engineer Park itself was at Punkabarri, from whence, owing to the scarcity of coolies, and the existing necessity of employing them in the conveyance of commissariat stores, its speedy removal was problematical.

4. Collecting therefore on the spot such tools as the executive engineer and the bazaar could supply me with, I directed Lieut. Pierson to proceed to Goke, to make a road from that post to the point selected on the Rumaam by myself and Lieut. Pierson, at which to cross, and to collect all material, and construct a timber bridge at that spot.

5. How Lieut. Pierson performed the task committed to his sole charge will be hereafter referred to.

6. You are aware that I was obliged to abandon the first intention of crossing the Great Rungeet by a bridge of casks, owing to the paucity of such of a favourable size, and because those of smaller dimensions had been rendered unavailable by their being riddled with holes perforated by a worm.

7. It was necessary to prepare rafts on shore to allow of short exposure to the fire of the enemy, when the bridge should be required. On the 29th January I proceeded to the Great Rungeet, tested, with the assistance of Captain Baker and Lieut. Beavan, with the Sikhs and sappers,

a raft peculiarly made of bamboos, and found that such, thus constructed, would support sixteen men; it merely remained, therefore, to adapt this material so as to ensure its bearing a greater weight. Orders were issued to Lieut. Beavan, of the Sebundy Sappers, to collect bamboos at the Rungeet, and coolies were despatched for cane, with which and by which the rafts were to be tied and guided. A small field work, to be made of gabions, was also ordered by me to protect the guard for defence of working party employed in throwing the bridge across. On the 31st January the Engineer Park, composed of seventy coolies and five Sirdars, moved down to the Great Rungeet, and I found that the field work had been completed by Lieut. Beavan. The sapper and miner serjeants not having arrived, Serjeant Dunne, of the Sebundy Sappers, was placed in charge of these men as park serjeant.

8. On the 1st I commenced making the rafts, being sheltered by a high bank from the fire of the enemy. Towards the afternoon, at 3 P.M., the rafts being completed, I selected a place down which to slide them to the river bank. The enemy's fire becoming heavy, two rafts only remaining to be taken down, and it being your order that I was not to expose the working parties too much, I desisted from sending down these two.

On the 2nd, early in the morning, the two remaining rafts were placed alongside the others. A demonstration on our part, by the fire of artillery and musketry, being made, I commenced moving the rafts near to the site selected for the bridge, and lacing the first two rafts together, floated them into their proper position; the other rafts, three in number, were then gradually lowered down to the causeway thus made, and were hauled into position. The bridge was sufficiently completed by about one o'clock to allow of troops being crossed.

9. As regards these operations, I particularly bring to

your notice, for favourable consideration, Captain Baker, from whom I received the greatest assistance, and Lieuts. Wanchope and Hawes, who also rendered willing aid. Of Lieut. Beavan, who was in command of the Sebundy Sappers at the Rungeet, who for a month previously had been erecting a bridge over the Rungnoo, making roads, and collecting material for these rafts, I cannot write too highly, and Lieut. Hidyat Alli, of Baker's Sikhs, rendered that personal assistance, and so encouraged and showed his men how to work as to draw on himself the applause of all present.

10. The bridge of rafts was 120 feet in length and 10 in width; it was strengthened, and strong guy canes were attached. The appearance was that of strength and lightness.

11. Lieut. Beavan, with a working party of Sebundy Sappers and of the Engineer Park, was employed on the road between the Rungeet and Mikh, not in making a good road, but in removing any obstacles, and widening it in such places as to allow of the safe passage of cattle. Arriving at Mikh, some of the men of the sappers and of the park were employed in cutting a new path up the steep hill towards Namchi, as the existing path was exceedingly bad, being simply a track. Parties of the Sebundy Sappers and of the Engineer Park were left by me to complete a traversable path between Mikh and Namchi, and I proceeded with force to Namchi on 9th February.

12. From that date up to the 15th, the Engineer Park and a portion of the Sebundy Sappers, with the aid of the Sikhs, were employed in making a road from Namchi to Sandoopchi (up an exceedingly steep ascent), in preparing a store-shed for the commissariat, and in collecting material, &c., for a block-house. I may here mention that the absence of proper tools in the Engineer Park was almost a stumbling-block to this work, as I had only one saw and one chisel

E. Stanford, Charing Cross

CAPTAIN IMPEYS FLOATING BRIDGE AT THE RUNGEET.

in it. At Namchi, Serjeants Dickson and O'Hara, of the Bengal Sappers and Miners, arrived; Serjeant Dickson was appointed to the charge of the park, *vice* Serjeant Dunne, and Serjeant O'Hara was sent off to join Lieut. Pierson at Goke.

It being considered expedient that the road in our rear, *viz.* from the Rungeet to Namchi, where a commissariat depôt was formed, should be made sufficiently good so as to allow of cattle being employed in the conveyance of stores, Lieut. Beavan was appointed by you Assistant Field Engineer, and was deputed to carry out this work and to superintend the completion of the store there, and the block-house. Thirty-seven of the Sebundy Sappers and Miners were attached to him.

13. On the 14th I marched up to Sandoopchi, having sent the park coolies to Buckcheem, and proceeding through Buckcheem on the 15th, picked up thirty-six Sebundy Sappers, and reached Temi in the evening. I was obliged to leave my park behind, as there were not sufficient coolies with the column under my command to convey the requisite commissariat stores and the bedding of the men. Sliding down Mount Tendong, the summit of which, with snow lying there, we crossed, the Sebundy Sappers were employed cutting a passage for the mules: this delayed our march exceedingly.

14. Whilst halting at Temi, I employed the park coolies and Sebundies in preparing the road down to the Teesta for the mules, and in making a road to the spring of water at Temi.

15. When I reached Radoong Ghât, on the 24th February, a place in which you determined on crossing the Teesta, I examined the river, and selected the most suitable site at which to construct the bridge. Half of the 25th was comparatively lost unfortunately. Parties of the Sebundy Sappers were sent with park coolies to cut timbers

and bamboos, the cane for tying having been previously collected by park coolies, whilst we halted on the 22nd, 23rd, and 24th at Linsing Ghât. On the 26th, 27th, up to 4 P.M. on the afternoon of the 28th, parties of H.M. 6th, of the Sikhs, Sebundy Sappers, and park coolies were employed in conveying, cutting timber and bamboos, in forming and in completing the bridge. The number of workmen employed the three and a half days was 520; the total number of working hours was 28. The bridge was in length 220 feet, in width, average of 8; there were six piers and one abutment (excluding from the calculation two rocks which served as piers); the height of made piers of stone averaged 6 feet; the two largest spans from rock to rock, and from the latter to shore, were 41 and 35 feet; the timbers thrown across these were 53 and 45 feet in length. There was no tackle to assist in moving such large timbers; *some of them were cut a quarter of a mile up the stream, and floated down, and the stream was running at the rate of at least fourteen miles an hour between the rocks. I have not heard of, nor have I read of, any bridge of this size having been constructed within so short a space of time, bearing in mind that no material lay at the spot, and that all had to be cut, and nearly all had to be brought on shoulders.*

16. Most conspicuous was Lieut. Hidyat Alli, of Baker's Sikhs, in the assistance he afforded me, not only by encouraging his men to emulate himself, but also by his ability in devising fresh, and improving on many, devices which I had suggested. I should be wanting in my duty to you if I did not bring him conspicuously to your notice, to enable you to do justice to him. All the parties of troops employed at this bridge most cordially endeavoured to promote a speedy completion of this work; otherwise it could not have been accomplished in so remarkably, and I may truly add marvellously, short time.

17. At the Teesta I left a portion of my park establish-

ment, some Sebundy Sappers, and some tools under Serjeant Dunne. Serjeant Dickson erected a small guard at the bridge head, and Serjeant Dunne, at the request of Major Platt, of H.M. 6th Foot (who commanded the post at the Teesta on our departure), threw up on the plateau above the bridge a stone work with an embrasure in it.

18. On our journey to Tumloong, the sappers, and a few of the engineer establishment remaining with me, were constantly employed in preparing portions of the way before us; so that we have left behind us, between Radoong Ghât and Kabee, a road easily to be traversed, excepting at the Munnudee, and even that portion has been much improved by the sappers.

19. Whilst waiting our departure from Tumloong, I sent orders to Serjeant Dunne, at your request, to make a road from Buckcheem, round Mount Tendong, down to Linsing Ghât, in order that the whole route from the Great Rungeet down to the Teesta River at that point might become a good hill road. When I passed by the old road from our first encamping ground at the Teesta, I found Serjeant Dunne's party at work at a very fair road down to Linsing Ghât; but a small portion had to be completed. The road up to Temi was a very good one; from thence up to Buckcheem the road, excepting round Mount Tendong, is not good; this is, however, accounted for by the nature of the soil and the constant moisture arising from the thickness of the jungle, the sun hardly ever penetrating it.

20. From Buckcheem to Sandoopchi the road is much better; from Sandoopchi to Namchi the road is very good, considering the want of width of ridge and the steepness.

21. At Namchi I found an exceedingly good store-shed, 100 feet in length and 25 feet wide; the block-house was completed excepting the thatching of roof. I do not con-

sider that the latter work has been carried on with the energy with which it should have been.

22. The road from Namchi to the Great Rungeet is an exceedingly good road, and, with slight annual repairs, will continue so for many years.

23. In the beginning of this paper I mentioned that I would further allude to Lieut. Pierson's services. Lieut. Pierson had not been three months in this country when he was ordered to join your force — was therefore unversed in the language, in truth was "*au bout de son* "*Latin*." He set to work with a determination to conquer all difficulties, and has most admirably succeeded; unaided at first, until Serjeant O'Hara joined him, with only the refuse of the sappers at his disposal, these men scarcely comprehending him, he conquered the tenacity of those who had been solely accustomed to construct bridges of a local standard, and succeeded in throwing over the Rumaam one which reflects great credit on himself, and shows what ability combined with energy can effect. Whilst carrying out this work, though short absences therefrom resulted in absurd mistakes being committed by these men, still he succeeded in constructing, with about fifty-three of the 73rd N.I., about 11 miles of excellent road to the river Rummam, and thence towards Rinchingpoong. Ordered to join your force, and accompanying the same from the Teesta to Darjeeling, he has secured a survey of the ground traversed by you, and thus has materially added to the knowledge and information desired; and this, together with the excellent survey and sketches of Lieut. Carter, of the Engineers, taken of the country through which we marched on Tumloong, will be valuable, being as correct and as clear a map of those portions of the country as could be produced by anyone with the means, opportunities, and time at their command.

24. In conclusion, I would bring to your favourable

notice the services of Serjeants Dickson and O'Hara, of the Bengal Sappers and Miners; Serjeant Dickson in my presence, and Serjeant O'Hara in that of Lieut. Pierson, having performed their duties to our satisfaction.

25. I herewith forward the map referred to.

I have, &c.,

ARCHIBALD IMPEY, Captain.
Field Engineer to the Sikhim Field Force.

Extract from Treaty between the Viceroy of India and Sikeong Kuzoo, Maharajah of Sikhim, signed by the latter at Tumloong, on the 28th March, 1861, and ratified by H.E. the Viceroy and Governor-General of India, at Calcutta, on the 16th April, 1861.

Whereas the continued depredations and misconduct of the officers and subjects of the Maha Rajah of Sikhim, and the neglect of the Maha Rajah to afford satisfaction for the misdeeds of his people, have resulted in an interruption, for many years past of the harmony which previously existed between the British Government and the Government of Sikhim, and have ultimately led to the invasion and conquest of Sikhim by a British force: And whereas the Maha Rajah of Sikhim has now expressed his sincere regret for the misconduct of his servants and subjects, his determination to do all in his power to obviate future misunderstanding, and his desire to be again admitted into friendship and alliance with the British Government, it is hereby agreed as follows :—

(The first seven clauses relate to payment of the fine imposed, and to the maintenance of good conduct for the future.)

8. The Government of Sikhim, from this date, abolishes all restrictions on travellers and monopolies in trade between the British territories and Sikhim. There shall henceforth be a free reciprocal intercourse and full liberty of commerce between the subjects of both countries; it shall be lawful for British subjects to go into any part of Sikhim for the purpose of travel or trade, and the subjects of all countries shall be permitted to reside in and pass through Sikhim, and to expose their goods for sale at any place and in any

manner that may best suit their purpose, without any interference whatever, except as is hereinafter provided.

9. The Government of Sikhim engages to afford protection to all travellers, merchants, or traders of all countries, whether residing in, trading in, or passing through Sikhim. If any merchant, traveller, or trader, being a European subject, shall commit any offence contrary to the laws of Sikhim, such person shall be punished by the representative of the British Government resident at Darjeeling, and the Sikhim Government will at once deliver such offender over to the British authorities for this purpose, and will on no account detain such offender in Sikhim on any pretext or pretence whatever. All other British subjects residing in the country to be liable to the laws of Sikhim; but such persons shall on no account be punished with loss of limb, or maiming, or torture, and every case of punishment of a British subject shall be at once reported to Darjeeling.

10. No duties or fees of any sort shall be demanded by the Sikhim Government of any person or persons on account of goods exported into the British territories from Sikhim, or imported into Sikhim from the British territories.

11. On all goods passing into or out of Thibet, Bhotan, or Nepaul, the Government of Sikhim may levy a duty of customs according to such a scale as may from time to time be determined and published, without reference to the destination of the goods, provided, however, that such duty shall on no account exceed 5 per cent. on the value of the goods at the time and place of the levy of the duty. On the payment of the duty aforesaid, a pass shall be given exempting such goods from liability to further payment on any account whatever.

12. With the view to protect the Government of Sikhim from fraud on account of under valuation for assessment of duty, it is agreed that the customs officers shall have the

option of taking over for the Government any goods at the value affixed on them by the owner.

13. In the event of the British Government desiring to open out a road through Sikhim with the view of encouraging trade, the Sikhim Government will raise no objection thereto, and will afford every protection and aid to the party engaged in the work. If a road is constructed, the Government of Sikhim undertakes to keep it in repair, and to erect and maintain suitable travellers' rest-houses throughout its route.

14. If the British Government desires to make either a topographical or geological survey of Sikhim, the Sikhim Government will raise no objection to this being done, and will afford protection and assistance to the officers employed in this duty.

15. Inasmuch as many of the late misunderstandings have had their foundation in the custom which exists in Sikhim of dealing in slaves, the Government of Sikhim binds itself from this date to punish severely any person trafficking in human beings, or seizing persons for the purpose of using them as slaves.

16. Henceforth the subjects of Sikhim may transport themselves, without let or hindrance, to any country to which they may wish to remove. In the same way the Government of Sikhim has authority to permit the subjects of other countries, not being criminals or defaulters, to take refuge in Sikhim.

17. The Government of Sikhim engages to abstain from any acts of aggression or hostility against any of the neighbouring States, which are allies of the British Government. If any disputes or questions arise between the people of Sikhim and those of neighbouring States, such disputes or questions shall be referred to the arbitration of the British Government, and the Sikhim Government agrees to abide by the decision of the British Government.

18. The whole military force of Sikhim shall join and afford every aid and facility to British troops when employed in the hills.

19. The Government of Sikhim will not cede or lease any portion of its territory to any other State without the permission of the British Government.

20. The Government of Sikhim engages that no armed force belonging to any other country shall pass through Sikhim without the sanction of the British Government.

21. (With reference to the seizure of certain criminals who had fled to Bhootan.)

22. (The Rajah to reside nine months of the year in Sikhim instead of in Thibet.)

23. (Copies of the Treaty in English, Nagree, and Bhooteate, exchanged, signed, and sealed.)

MEMORANDUM by COLONEL GAWLER and DR. ARCHIBALD CAMPBELL, late SUPERINTENDENT OF DARJEELING, accompanying the MEMORIAL presented on 25th April, 1873, by the DEPUTATION OF THE SOCIETY OF ARTS, AT THE INDIA OFFICE, TO HIS GRACE THE DUKE OF ARGYLL, SECRETARY OF STATE FOR INDIA, on the subject of Facilitating our Communication through India with Central Asia.

The State of Sikhim affords special facilities for opening commercial relations with Thibet, Central Asia, and Western China.

1. Because there has always existed among one section of the people a very friendly disposition towards the British Government, and among the remainder, or ruling portion, there exists towards us a real respect of a very wholesome nature, owing to the success of the expedition of 1861, and to the exemplary behaviour of the troops (as testified by the British Envoy), which left on their minds no feelings of apprehension, irritation, or resentment.

2. Because it is the shortest and most direct route to Lhassa from British territory, and there is already a road from Darjeeling to the Thibet frontier, practicable for pack-animals, and a pass (the Chola) 14,900 feet high, open nearly all the year round, and free from snow for six months in the year. By a branch extension of the East Indian Railway to the foot of the Darjeeling hills, the transport of Indian and English goods intended for Thibet, as well as our Darjeeling tea trade, would be greatly facilitated.

3. Because the Treaty of 1861, between the British Government and Sikhim, establishes free trade between the

subjects of the two Governments, free permission for the British Government to survey the country, and to make or improve roads in it, which the Sikhim Government are to keep in order if made.

4. Because of the intimate connections between Sikhim and Thibet, as follows :—

The head of the Sikhim religion (Budhism) is in Thibet; the Sikhim Rajah's mother is a Thibetean; many of the Sikhim officials are Thibeteans; the Sikhim Rajah receives a salary from Thibet, and, together with the Sikhim officials, spends most of his time in Thibet, at Choombi.

5. On account of the close proximity to the Sikhim frontier (about three hours) of the Thibetean town of Choombi, which is a large market town with bazaars, and whence there is a good road to Lhassa.*

With the advantages, physical and political, above enumerated, it is apprehended that there could be no great difficulty in establishing a consular agency at Choombi to begin with, and eventually in sending an envoy to Lhassa as soon as our Treaty with China has been patiently and thoroughly made known and discussed, and when the people of Thibet have become better acquainted with us.

PROBABLE TRADE WITH THIBET.

* "If commercial intercourse is more fairly established, " it is certain that a very considerable trade will spring up " between Thibet and Bengal. They will give gold, silver, " ponies, musk, borax, wool, turquoise, silk, and munjeet, " for broadcloths, bleached goods, tobacco, and pearls."—Hon. A. Eden, to Secretary to Government, Bengal. No. 40, 8th April, 1861, para. 36.